Orchids
in a Garden City

Orchids
in a Garden City

TEOH Eng Soon

Marshall Cavendish Editions

Editor: Melvin Neo
Designers: Bernard Go Kwang Meng/Teoh Eng Soon
Published by Marshall Cavendish Editions
An imprint of Marshall Cavendish International
1 New Industrial Road, Singapore 536196

Other Marshall Cavendish Offices
Marshall Cavendish International. PO Box 65829, London EC1P 1NY, UK • Marshall Cavendish Corporation. 99 White Plains Road, Tarrytown NY 10591-9001, USA • Marshall Cavendish International (Thailand) Co Ltd. 253 Asoke, 12th Flr, Sukhumvit 21 Road, Klongtoey Nua, Wattana, Bangkok 10110, Thailand • Marshall Cavendish (Malaysia) Sdn Bhd, Times Subang, Lot 46, SubangHi-Tech Industrial Park, Batu Tiga, 40000 Shah Alam, Selangor Darul Ehsan, Malaysia.

National Library Board, Singapore Cataloguing-in-Publication Data
Teoh, Eng-Soon, 1938-
Orchids in a garden city / Teoh Eng Soon. – Singapore : Marshall Cavendish Editions, c2010.
p. cm.
Includes bibliographical references.
ISBN-13 : 978-981-4276-73-3
1. Orchids – Singapore. 2. Orchids – Singapore – Pictorial works. I. Title.
QK495.O64
584.4095957—dc22 OCN609784443

Printed in Malaysia by Times Offset Printing

Contents

Dedication

For Phaik Khuan, John, Kristine, Chrissy and Ning

Preface

Orchids in a Garden City has the ring of an oxymoron. Yet in bustling Singapore many roadside trees are festooned with orchids growing in their natural state, not fussed over, and blooming in abundance in response to periodic thunderstorms. They have done so for decades, if not for centuries: and not just the ubiquitous Pigeon Orchid, but also *Bulbophyllums, Grammatophyllums* and the occasional *Cymbidium*. As part of its conservation effort, the Singapore Botanic Gardens' dedicated orchid group has attached some 3,000 plants of indigenous orchid species to trees at the roadside, in parks and in nature reserves.

Singapore was an entreport for the transshipment of thousands, perhaps even millions of orchid plants to Europe since the orchid plundering heydays of the nineteenth century, and in the late twentieth century to America, Japan and even to some African nations. It was unavoidable that some attempt would be made to grow the many varied species locally. After some trial and error, Singapore gardeners concentrated on the hardy, free flowering species and eventually this resulted in a selective interest in *Dendrobium*, *Spathoglottis*, the Scorpion Orchids, *Vanda, Paraphalaenopsis* and *Phalaenopsis*. Singapore-bred hybrids produced over the past eighty years are concentrated in such genera. Some nurseries, inspired by the Coolhouse in the Singapore Botanic Gardens have recently constructed coolhouses of their own and are now offering a wide range of cool-growing orchids. Growers with space constraints prefer to focus on miniature species. So the range broadens.

Generally, the orchid scene is dominated by the orchid hybrids that Singapore and its neighbours have produced for the flower trade. These orchids are everywhere. The moment one steps into Singapore, one is greeted by splendid landscaped or grouped displays of beautiful orchids in the airport terminals. One sees them again in the hotels, in shopping

LEFT: Dendrobium farmeri.

malls, offices, and along the roadside. In Singapore, one can derive much pleasure, at little cost, by taking an interest in orchids. At the Botanic Gardens, during Orchid Meetings or Shows, and in nurseries and private collections, one will encounter the species.

This is not a book about Singapore's native flora, nor will it attempt to detail how orchids are best cultivated. Instead I have chosen to feature the orchids that have caught my eye during my visits to numerous gardens and shows, and how they appear at different times of the day.

The brief descriptions convey the thoughts and memories that arose in my mind when I saw these orchids.

I am learning to see *heaven in a wild flower*, and wish the reader would do the same. The joy is almost for free.

Teoh Eng Soon
Singapore, March 2010

LEFT: The distinctive part of an orchid flower. *ABOVE: Vanda* Fuch's Delight.

Orchids in the Garden City of Singapore: *Ehi-Pasiko*

The phrase *ehi pasiko* is in Pali. It means 'come and see for yourself'. It is an invitation. It is neutral statement but it does imply that if one does not come and see, one will miss a lot. That is the way I choose to describe the orchids in Singapore. In this book I wish to share the pleasure that I have derived during the 50 years that I have spent admiring the orchids in this country. It covers only a small portion of the orchid wealth. The selection is guided by personal preference and my admiration for specific flowers.

Singapore is located in a region which naturalists call Malesia, an area so rich in tropical flora that it nutures tens of thousands of orchid species. Our small island state is home to possibly 220 orchid species in 75 genera. Many species are modest with their flowers but it is possible to witness a spectacular flowering of a species if one keeps a lookout for it. A couple of orchid species that have established themselves on roadside trees flower gregariously several days after a thunderstorm: at this time, wafted fragrance emanates from the ephemeral Pigeon Orchid. In 1893, the spectacular, free bloomer *Vanda* Miss Joaquim made its maiden appearance in the Singapore garden of Agnes Joaquim. Anyone who has visited Hawaii would be familiar with the Aloha orchid: *Vanda* Miss Joaquim by any other name is happy throughout the tropics and always generous with its pretty flowers. Soon after the end of the Second World War, when my mother thought that it was safe to beautify our home, she planted a few rows of Miss Joaquim's *Vanda*. It was not too expensive, and it was reliable. What it required was plenty of sunlight, the more the better, together with water and fertilizer. Today, this *Vanda* is Singapore's National Flower.

Let us begin by looking at some native species, and a small sampling of other species that were imported from the surrounding region when orchids became a passion in these parts. During our sojourn, we need to be aware that what we see today are the much improved specimens obtained through line breeding and selection. They may be quite different from the clones available to the pioneers of the early twentieth century. A number of important stud plants and hybrids are still in cultivation and we can look at them before going on to see the results of recent breeding programmes, landscaped orchids, orchid shows and other aspects of orchids.

The way to enjoy orchids is by admiring their good qualities, and unless one is planning to be a hybridizer, to forget about searching for their faults. One should be prepared to examine them both with one's eyes and mind (an eye for beauty, and a bank of knowledge), to look in unusual places, at different times of the day and at different months of the year. Even a faded flower has its charm.

ABOVE: Vanda Kwa Geok Choo was bred by the Singapore Botanic Gardens and named for Mrs. Lee Kuan Yew.

PAGES 14 & 15: Vanda Miss Joaquim, the national flower of Singapore.

ACRIOPSIS FROM THE GREEK *AKRIS* (LOCUST) *OPSIS* (APPEARANCE)

As the light recedes is the garden, the tiny flowers of *Acriopsis javanica* appear like a swarm of tiny insects hovering above a small epiphyte. Although its flowers are not spectacular, the *Acriopsis* makes an attractive focus if planted on a tree trunk where it can be easily noticed. The common variety has yellowish petals and sepals streaked with purple, a colour repeated on the lip. This lowland orchid is common from Tenasserim to Papua New Guinea.

ABOVE: Acriopsis indica.

CALANTHE: *KALOS* (Greek: BEAUTIFUL) *ANTHE* (FLOWER)

Calanthe triplicata is abundant in freshwater swamp forests in neighbouring Malaysia. It enjoys a wide distribution from India across Southeast Asia to the Pacific Islands, growing from sea level to 1,700 metres. It flowers all year round. It is a pity that this lovely orchid is not being propagated and cultivated as a garden ornamental.

LEFT: Arundina bambusifolia, the Bamboo Orchid occurs in open scrub, *belukar*, and on hill slopes up to 1,500 metres throughout Southeast Asia. It is a popular garden flower.

ABOVE: Dwarf strain of *Arundina*.

WILD AND FREE

People have generally left these two local orchids alone and they thrive in the wild, uncollected.

LEFT: Cymbidium finlaysonianum is a common sight on country roads in Southeast Asia. With thick leathery leaves that measure 75 cm by 4 cm, it forms large clumps on trees or rocks in exposed places. The pendulous, metre-long inflorescence carries two dozen, well spaced, yellow to chocolate coloured flowers that are streaked with red. In a large garden or a tree it makes a striking focal point. *(Photographed in the unique garden of Drs. Esau & Anjula Thomas.)*

ABOVE: Plocoglottis lowii is an unusual terrestrial orchid with purple pseudobulbs and long pointed leaves which are greenish purple on the upper surface and bright purple underneath. The inflorescence is generally long and arching, with up to 20 buds, but they open one at a time. *P. lowii* is widespread in damp, shaded, coastal, lowland forests from the Andaman Islands and Thailand through Malaysia to Indonesia.

UNCOMMON ORCHID FLOWERS

ABOVE: Macodes petola is a famous Southeast Asian jewel orchid which grows in the damp humus covering rocks near streams. The greenish or purplish leaves with their golden veins are the attractive feature of the plant. They are a collector's item and have their own microclimate requirements. One should not miss the opportunity to admire their flowers because the plants are generally not well grown enough for them to bloom. But they are small and easily overlooked.

RIGHT: Schoenorchis fragrans is a possibly the smallest vandaceous orchid species. A full grown plant is barely 3 cm to 4 cm across and often not much taller but it produces masses of tiny, pink flowers when well grown, The species is native to Indochina and needs a cool environment to do well. The Miniature Section of a Singapore Orchid Show is one place where one might possibly see it in bloom.

BULBOPHYLLUMS

As their name suggests, these epiphytic orchids are readily identified by the plump pseudobulbs which carry a single leaf near the tip and a terminal flower or inflorescence. The flowers come in many shapes, but they all possess a hinged lip which causes an insect to tumble head down into the spur when it tries to sip the nectar. (The lips are shown in close-up overleaf). The three species illustrated here are native to Singapore and Malaysia.

ABOVE: Bulbophyllum (Cirrhopetalum) vaginatum is a common orchid found growing on old trees in the Tanglin-Bukit Timah area of Singapore. The plants are short but they establish huge colonies that practically cover the trunk and main branches of the trees above a man's reach. They flower gregariously in response to a pronounced dip in temperature.

RIGHT: Bulbophyllum (Cirrhopetalum) medusae.

PAGES 26 & 27: Bulbophyllum auratum.

BULBOPHYLLUM LION KING

The *Bulbophyllum* Lion King which is a present from my friend Syed Yusof Alsagoff flowers regularly in my garden. It grows attached to a pine tree. Late one evening I caught a glimpse of its solitary bloom lit by the setting sun. I moved a young stag horn to give some drama to the background because I had photographed this orchid before and needed a new perspective. The result is rather delightful (*left*).

A few days later when the flowers had withered I took another photograph, this time allowing the evening breeze to move the flowers (*above*).

EXPLOSIVE FLOWERING FOLLOWING SUNLESS SKIES

Coelogyne rochussenii is widely distributed from Sumatra to the Philippines and it is a common lowland orchid in Peninsular Malaysia. This clone is special because it is a family heirloom of Mak Chin On, one of the most successful commercial orchid growers in Singapore. He received his plant from his father-in-law who had inherited it from his father: thus the clone had been passed down for nearly a hundred years. Mak grew several propagations in pots which he hung at different locations in his two-hectare farm in Seletar, and it flowered for him indifferently for many years.

In 1994 a huge forest fire aggravated by smoke from slash-and-burn agriculture in Sumatra blanketed Singapore and the west coast of Peninsular Malaysia with smog for months. Blue skies and fluffy clouds totally disappeared. When the winds changed and the rains came in late November the sky cleared. Suddenly Mak found that every single pot of his *Coelogyne* was producing thousands of blooms. The exact stimuli which result in such massive displays in orchids remain a mystery, but they are well worth investigating.

In its natural habitat, *C. rochussenii* grows on tree trunks near rivers and lakes. The flowers emit a faint smell of lemon.

LEFT: Coelogyne species with linear petals. *ABOVE:* Mak Chin On's *Coelogyne rochussenii.*

LEFT: Coelogyne mayeriana is a lowland terrestrial orchid distributed from Sumatra eastwards to Borneo and Java. It is found in lowland forests and sometimes on limestone. The flowers resemble those of the so-called Black Orchid, *Coelogyne pandurata*, from which it is distinguished by the absence of a claw on the midlobe of its lip. Although this orchid is native to Singapore, it is not commonly cultivated because its flowers are not long-lasting.

THE LARGEST ORCHID IN THE WORLD

Grammatophyllum speciosum, the Tiger Orchid, is the largest orchid in the world, by sheer mass or the total surface area of its flowers. A plant collected in 1890 in Selangor by the renowned orchid hunter, William Micholitz who worked for Sanders, was said to have weighed over a ton, and had to be divided before it could be shipped. Half was given to the Singapore Botanic Gardens; that plant is still thriving, and in bloom at this very moment of writing (June 2009), with 16 sprays in one clump. The other half was sent to the Colombian Exposition in Chicago where it created a sensation. The plant was eventually presented to the Royal Botanic Gardens at Kew, and their records showed that this was the biggest orchid plant they ever received. During the World Orchid Conference in 1963, the Kebun Istana (the Palace Gardens of the Sultan of Johor) used a 10-ton lorry to move its clump of the Tiger Orchid to exhibit in the Festival Show.

The Tiger Orchid usually grows in the crotch of a large tree or on the ground, and its arching canes may reach a length of 3 metres, with 20 narrow leaves 50-60 cm long x 3-4 cm wide. Most plants in cultivation have shorter canes although they may be numerous and a good clump can still produce 50 sprays with 2,000 to 3,000 flowers simultaneously, each 10 cm across. The Tiger Orchid is said to be an infrequent bloomer, flowering only once in two to three years though of late mature plants seem to bloom annually. No one fully understands the conditions for flower spike initiation, but a spell of dry weather appears to be necessary. The species has a wide distribution from Myanmar to Thailand, Vietnam, Cambodia, Malaysia, Singapore and Indonesia to Papua New Guinea, that is, if one considers *Grammatophyllum papuanum* to be a variety of *G. speciosum*.

Grammatophyllum speciosum was found in Tuas and Ubin in the early twentieth century, and at Bukit Timah in the 1980s. The Singapore Botanic Gardens has made an excellent effort to reintroduce the Tiger Orchid into the island's natural flora and one can see clumps of this orchid even on the roadside trees in the busy shopping boulevards. They have yet to bloom.

ABOVE: Grammatophyllum speciosum. The name *Grammatophyllum* is derived from Greek *gramma* (letter) and *phyllon* (leaf) referring to the conspicuous marking on the petals and sepals that look rather like letters. Apart from Tiger Orchid, it has other native names: in Malay it is known as *Bunga puteri* (Princess Flower); *Bunga bidadari* (Nymph's Flower). In Thailand it is called *Wan phetchahueng.* This photograph shows the flowers of the original plant collected by Micholitz in 1890 and now thriving in the Singapore Botanic Gardens. The flowers are fuller than most varieties.

A MORE MANAGABLE *GRAMMATOPHYLLUM*

Grammatophyllum scriptum is a smaller species. A native of Indonesia and the Philippines, it has a long string of names both scientific (in botanical jargon, synonyms) and local. Synonyms: *G. multiflorum* Lindley; *Angraecum scriptum* Rumphius; *Helleborine mollucca* Rumphius; *G. leopardinum* Reichenbach. Different Indonesian islands have their own local native names for the orchid: *Bunga Bidadari; Anggerik Bidadari*; *Angrec Calappa* (it grew on coconut palms), *Angrec Lida*; *Angrek Boki, Bonga Boki, Bonga Putri; Saja Baki; Bunga Puteri ; Anggerik Puteri*; *Anggerik Matjan; Anggerik Harimau; Anggerik Boki*; *Anggerik Garingsing*; *Anggerik Tiwu, Anggerik Susuru*; *Saja Bake; Saja Ngawa ; Saja Ngawan*; *Tijgerorchidee.*

Obviously a beautiful and much admired orchid, this species grows into large specimen plants when attached to trees, annually producing thousands of flowers on metre-long, arching inflorescences. The pseudobulbs are cone-shaped, rounded at base, green, with a few long, narrow, thin leaves. Stiff white roots grow outwards and upwards all round the plant, typical of the genus, and very striking in this species. The flowers of the common variety are 5 cm across, of a light brownish green, marked with brownish patches (appearing rather like tiger skin; hence var. *tigrinum* or *G. leopardinum*), while those of the *alba* variety are plain apple green. Geogius Everhardus Rumphius (1627–1702) gave a long account of its medicinal usage in Amboin.

ABOVE & RIGHT: Grammatophyllum scriptum, var. *alba* in a small landscape.

ABOVE & RIGHT: Dendrobium secundum. An inflorescence of this common, lowland, coastal species looks rather like a comb. The species is distributed from Tenasserim to Indochina and down Malaysia to Indonesia and the Philippines. The white variety is less common then the red.

ERIA

These are the poor cousins of the *Dendrobium* because their flowers do not last beyond a few days. They would otherwise be popular as some species produce a good spray of attractive flowers, and some are fragrant. *Eria* is a large genus with around 400 species, with 48 in Peninsular Malaysia and at least 20 in Singapore.

LEFT: Eria oblitterata is a mountain species growing at 800–2,400 metres in Indonesia, Malaysia, Cambodia and Vietnam. It is frequently in bloom at the Coolhouse of the Singapore Botanic Gardens.

ABOVE: Eria xanthocheila is a lowland species with spectacular branching inflorescences.

ANOTHER LOWLAND *ERIA*

LEFT: Eria floribunda. This lovely *Eria* is a common lowland epiphyte throughout Southeast Asia. EJH Corner and CE Carr collected it from the freshwater swamp-forest in Jurong in 1932. A strong plant may carry several densely flowered inflorescences simultaneously. The white of the flowers is accentuated by a red anther cap.

Corner was Assistant Director of the Singapore Botanic Gardens from 1929 to 1941 and became Professor of Tropical Botany at Cambridge University in 1966. His *Wayside Trees of Malaya* is a classic. Carr managed rubber estates in Malacca and Pahang from 1919 to 1931 during which time he accompanied Holttum and Corner on their plant expeditions. His collection of orchids deposited in Singapore numbers 4,300. He joined the Kew Herbarium in 1933. The following year during a collecting expedition in Papua New Guinea he contracted blackwater fever, and died at a premature age of 44.

TERRESTRIAL ORCHIDS

Singapore and Malaysia are home to some lovely terrestrial orchids.

ABOVE: Eulophia herbracea

RIGHT: Eulophia spectabilis

ORCHIDS FROM A BYGONE ERA

These two orchids are not commonly cultivated in gardens today.

ABOVE: Bromheadia finlaysoniana, a common lowland orchid with ephemeral flowers.

RIGHT: Arachnis flos-aeries var. insignis, the Black Spider Orchid.

Orchid Pollinators

Colourful orchids are pollinated by bees but these insects do not enjoy the colour spectrum seen by the human eye. Their visual range is ultra-violet. Colours appear as patterns to the bees. Scent is an important attractant for bees and different species are attracted by different fragrances. The *Xylocarpa* or Carpenter Bee, formerly ubiquitous in Singapore, is an indiscriminate pollinator and will visit many flowers, among them, most species of *Vanda* and *Phalaenopsis*, as well as the common Straits Rhododendron *(Malestoma malabrathicum).* Natural hybrids occur in many orchid genera (*Ophrys* and *Dactylorhizia* in Europe, *Calanthe* in Japan, *Paphiopedilum* in Thailand and Vietnam, *Dendrobium* in Papua New Guinea, *Arachnis* in Malaysia, *Phalaenopsis* in Sumatra, and *Vanda* in Singapore and Malaysia) because the insects do not discriminate between those species which occur in the same area and flower at the same time.

RIGHT: *Dendrobium smillieae* is the only Australian orchid known to be pollinated by a bird, the yellow honeyeater, *Lichenostomus flavus.* The clustered inflorescence of white flowers with their iridescent green lips is spectacular. It is a common lowland orchid in Northern Queensland and Papua New Guinea: it shares the same habitat as *D. lasianthera* in the latter region.

LEFT: Carpenter Bee feeding on a flower of a hybrid *Vanda* with *V. tricolor* in its background.

MOTHS AS POLLINATORS

White flowers are generally pollinated by moths.

ABOVE: Corymborkis veratrifolia is an attractive lowland shrub which is widespread in Peninsular Malaysia but generally ignored by gardeners. It has stout, woody stems of moderate height that carry several unstalked, tough, pleated, dark green leaves. Branching inflorescences with three white flowers per side branch arise from the axils of leaves near the top of the plant. The flowers are fragrant in the evening and are pollinated by a sphinged moth with a long proboscis.

RIGHT: Angraecum sesquipedale predicta. A three-word name is most unusual in botanical nomenclature, but this highlights the theory of evolution. When Charles Darwin saw the Madagascan white orchid with the 18 centimeter long spur, he predicted that a moth with a proboscis of equal length must exist for the flower to be pollinated. Only a tongue of that length could ever recover the nectar produced by the *Angraecum*. His prediction was treated with disbelief until such a moth was actually discovered. African orchids like the *Angraecums* are fairly new to Singapore but one will sometimes see a plant flowering in the gardens.

The Early Days

At the beginning of the twentieth century many gardening enthusiasts were ambivalent about the orchids which they planted in their Singapore garden. The good point about orchids was the fact that some orchid flowers lasted a long time, but this was not a universal characteristic. In some species the flowers were ephemeral (they lasted less than a day). Sometimes a plant had to be grown for many years before it would start to bloom. Many species were seasonal, or produced a poor show of flowers. Furthermore, some plants were large, and difficult to care for.

In 1928, Hans Burgeff, passing through Singapore following a visit to Bogor, showed Eric Holttum the method of seed sowing in sterile nutrient agar. He practically started a horticultural revolution. Soon Holttum, John Laycock, Tan Hoon Siang, Lee Kim Hong and their friends were all busy transferring pollen between orchid species, occasionally without regard to their genetic proximity. Several of the resultant hybrids surpassed their parents by blooming freely throughout the year, and producing numerous sprays of flowers that lasted for weeks or months. Using *Vanda* Miss Joaquim as a yardstick, these hybrids were judged to be as good with respect to hardiness, ease of cultivation and propagation and, most importantly, floriferousness. These are still the main qualities one expects of tropical orchids today. In those days growers were looking for plants that could tolerate full sun, were easy to handle, and not fussy about their needs. At that time, at the very most, one might construct a lath house to provide some shade, simulating the dappled sunlight enjoyed by epiphytes like the *Dendrobium* and *Phalaenopsis*. There were no cool houses.

The successful hybrids of those early days established the direction of orchid hybridization in Singapore. First to germinate and flower was *Spathoglottis* Primrose, the cross made at Penang Hill between the lowland *S. plicata* and the highland *S. aurea* in May 1929, seed sown at the Singapore Botanic Gardens (SBG) and flowered in August 1931. Two scarlet spider orchids, *Aranthera* Mohamed Haniff and *Aranthera* James Storie, raised by SBG flowered in 1936 and 1937: both were free flowering. Crosses between two species of *Arachnis* took a longer time to bloom, partly due to a poor choice of one parent. By chance, *Arachnis hookeriana* var. *luteola* was also used in hybridizing and this resulted in a series of free flowering, vigorous hybrids: *Arachnis* Ishbel, (flowered 1938), *A.* Maggie Oei (flowered 1940), and *A.* Catherine, (flowered 1942). Breeding *Arachnis* to *Vanda* resulted in the hybrid genus *Aranda* which carried compact inflorescences with durable flowers of excellent substance. *Aranda* Deborah (flowered 1938) led the way, followed by *A.* Nancy (flowered 1939) and *A.* Hilda Galistan (flowered 1940). Perhaps it was the War, but some *Aranda* took a very long time to flower: for instance, *Aranda* Lucy Laycock, once a prized cut-flower, flowered 13 years after seed sowing! Many hybrid *Vandas* made by van Brero, C.A Chevalier, the Mataram Estate and others in Java were imported into Singapore before World War II, and some constitute the backbone of many famous Singapore hybrids.

Breeding within the horn, cane, or *Spathulata Dendrobiums* and crossing them to the round *D. biggibum* (syn. *D. phalaenopsis*) produced excellent early hybrids which pointed another direction for Singaporean hybridizers. *Dendrobium* Louisae raised by Chavelier in Bandoeng showed that it was possible to cut down the pollination-flowering period to two and half years. *D.* Caesar, (1937), *D.* Pompadour (originated in France; repeated in Java 1937) *D.* Dang Toi (1941) were outstanding. Laycock's *D.* Constance (1941) highlighted the possibilities with the horn type.

After the War, Singapore emerged as a leading centre for orchid hybridization. It benefited from its proximity to the source of natural species, and also from the work of the early Dutch hybridizers in Java. In turn, Singapore inspired Rapee Sagarik who employed Thailand's rich orchid resource to turn the country into a premier producer of wonderful orchid hybrids and cut-flowers. While the Aloha Orchid (*Vanda* Miss Joaquim) also dazzled Hawaiian planters who cultivated it on a massive scale for use in leis, Hawaiian breeders never lost sight of their aim to produce the ultimate strap leaf *Vanda*: the improvements they made greatly benefited the Thais and the Singaporeans. Being only a tiny red dot on the world's map, Singapore had to be quick to take advantage of advancements made in other parts of the world, and along with the rest of Southeast Asia, we are grateful to Haruyuki Kamemoto for his contribution to *Dendrobiums*, the second component of the cut-flower industry.

A GOLDEN SHOWER INDEED

LEFT: The arches at the National Orchid Garden in the Singapore Botanic Gardens are decorated with *Oncidium* Goldiana var. Golden Shower which was raised by and flowered for the Gardens just before World War II. It was described and named as *Oncidium* Golden Shower in the *Malayan Orchid Review* of 1940. The eventual official hybrid name is Goldiana registered by Atherton from Honolulu with the Royal Horticultural Society and published in the *Orchid Review* in 1941. By the time Singapore learnt that its given name had no priority status, the name had stuck among the hobbyists and those involved with the florist trade. 'Golden Shower' is the third floriferous orchid produced in the early days and it is still a valuable cut-flower. It flowers throughout the year.

Identifying the Right White Scorpion Orchid

The flowering of *Arachnis* Maggie Oei achieved by John Laycock in 1940 through a remake of the crossing between *Arachnis hookeriana* var. *luteola* and *A. flos-aeries* was a major breakthrough in the production of free-flowering orchids for the tropics. An earlier crossing with the typical *alba* variety of *A hookeriana* had failed to flower but this time Laycock had chosen the var. *luteola* to make the hybrid. The lesson learnt, nobody wasted their time trying to breed with the common *alba* variety of *A. hookeriana* because it took five years or more to see the result of one's effort, and if the hybrid failed to bloom, too much time would have been wasted.

Arachnis hookeriana var. *luteola* was originally collected from Pulau Tekong and the east coast of Peninsular Malaysia, growing on sandy soil near the sea. It is a tough, compact monopodial, with an erect inflorescence 60 cm long, carrying 6-8 well spaced, creamy white flowers, 5.5 cm across. However, on a really vigorous plant the inflorescence may carry up to 10-15 flowers.

TOP RIGHT: Arachnis hookeriana var *luteola.*

ABOVE: Aranda Bertha Braga (*V. tricolor* x *A.* Maggie Oei, by SBG,1957). The spots are inherited from *V. tricolor.*

ABOVE: The floriferous *Arachnis* Maggie Oei (*A. hookeriana* var. *luteola* x *A. flos-aeries*) bred by John Laycock (1935) and raised in the Singapore Botanic Gardens, first flowered in November 1940. It pioneered Singapore's cut-flower industry. It was prolific, travelled well and regained its lustre after soaking in water. It is the parent of several outstanding multigeneric hybrids.

Inheritance Comes from Both Sides

The *Vanda* parent plays an important role when it comes to the coloration, size, form and arrangement of the resulting *Aranda*. *Vanda coerulea* in the background imparts a blue coloration and tessellations, *V. dearei* yellow, *V. lamellata* brown, *V. insignis* orange or salmon, and *V. tricolor* var. *sauvis* purple spots.

ABOVE: Vanda dearei. This large, clear yellow *Vanda* is in the bloodline of most sizable, clear yellow Scorpion Orchids, *Vanda*, and *Ascocenda*. It is pleasantly scented and some of its hybrids are fragrant.

RIGHT: Aranda Majula (*A.* Maggie Oei x *V. insignis,* by SBG, 1967) The spotting came from an *Arachnis* grandparent; *V. insignis* imparted the background colour.

THE EVER–BLOOMING *ARANDA*

Aranda, hybrids between *Arachnis* and *Vanda,* are the backbone of Singpore's orchid cut-flower industry. A good *Aranda* not only looks beautiful on the plant, it has to look good indoors in artificial light, and it must have a long vase life. Delicate, clear colours are an asset, and the flowers must have heavy substance, the stem stout and long. A related hybrid is the *Mokara* produced by crossing *Arachnis* or *Aranda* to the large, later generation *Ascocenda*.

ABOVE: A collection of *Aranda* readied for display. Each plant is about 80 cm tall and carries 3-4 sprays of flowers that are about 80 per cent open. While these plants are raised in full sunlight, they will stay fresh on the plants for three weeks indoors, but many display plants are changed every fortnight.

RIGHT: Aranda Baby Teoh is of delicate mauve.

FULLER FORM IN *ARANDAS*

Improved form was achieved either by backcrossing *Aranda* to strap leaf *Vanda*, or by breeding with a tetraploid *Vanda*. Backcrossing was difficult because a sterility barrier in *Aranda* from which very few, and only amphidiploid, clones escaped.

ABOVE: Aranda Tay Swee Eng (*Aranda* Lily Chong x *V.* Piha Moon) bred by C. C. Chong was the first second-generation *Aranda* to be much sought after. It has been mericloned and is still popular with the florist. There is only a small amount of *V. coerulea* in its make-up and more *V. sanderiana.* Hence, the more prominent tessellations, and less blue.

RIGHT: Aranda Noorah Alsagoff (*Arachnis hookeriana luteola* x *V.* Dawn Nishmura) bred by Syed Yusof Alsagoff is a first generation *Aranda* made with a tetraploid *Vanda* which has 50 per cent of *V. coerulea* in its make-up. This results in the dominant blue colour.

MERICLONING RESULTS IN COLOUR MUTATIONS

ABOVE: Aranda How Yee Peng named after its breeder is another second generation *Aranda* with a blue- violet colour derived from its pollen parent, the tetraploid *V.* Dawn Nishimura. This *Vanda* was used extensively to produce hybrids in Singapore. *Aranda* Noorah Alsagoff, *A.* How Yee Peng, *A.* Wong Bee Yeok and *A.* Ang Hee Seng all bred from Dawn share the same blue colour.

RIGHT: Aranda Ang Hee Seng, red form. The blue orchid was bred by Syed Yusof Alsagoff. Afterwards, from mericloning a red colour form emerged for this *Aranda*. It was more robust than the original and is a popular florist variety. Beautiful colour mutants are extremely common in *Dendrobium* and some mutants have also appeared in mericloned *Phalaenopsis* and *Dorittaenopsis*.

GOLDEN SPIDERS

Clear, pure yellow is very desirable colour in *Vanda* and it is derived from *Vanda dearei* which hails from Borneo. Alba clones of *V. sanderiana* increased the size of the hybrids while adding *Ascocentrum* reduced it. Golden coloured *Vanda* and *Ascocenda* were used to produce remarkably attractive *Aranda* and *Mokara* in Singapore and Thailand. *Vanda denisonniana* has also been used in breeding but size and flatness have yet to be achieved in its hybrids.

ABOVE: A bed of golden yellow *Aranda* at the Singapore Botanic Gardens.

RIGHT: Mokara Zaleha Zaleha Alsagoff. This is the only hybrid which has earned a First Class Certificate from the Orchid Society of South East Asia (see John Elliott, *Orchid Hybrids of Singapore 1893–2003,* cover pix, or Teoh Eng Soon, *Orchids of Asia*, 3rd ed., 2005, p. 315). The photograph does not show the FCC clone; nevertheless, this is an outstanding clone. The flowers are long lasting but the plant requires skillful handling.

ABOVE: Ascocenda Jakkit Gold, a complex fifth generation *Ascocenda* carrying the genes of *Vanda dearei, V. coerulea, V. sanderiana, V. tricolor,* and *V. luzonica. Vanda coerulea* intensifies the yellow of *V. dearei.*

SUN-LOVING SEMI-TERETE & QUARTER-TERETE *VANDAS*

From around 1932, growers, first in Java, then Singapore and Ceylon, learnt that breeding terete-leaf *Vanda* (now called *Papillionanthe*) to strap-leaf *Vanda* produced impressive, large, colourful, free-flowering, semi-terete *Vanda* that thrive in full sun. Presently, there is an opportunity to make better hybrids with the wide range of readily available, inexpensive, outstanding, modern, strap leaf *Vanda*. However, these large plants are more suited to a big garden, and it takes four years from pollination for the hybrid to bloom.

ABOVE: A quarter-terete *Vanda.*

QUARTER-TERETE *VANDA*

They enjoy full sun. They are perennial favourites because their flowers last for months on the plant.

ABOVE: Vanda Tan Chay Yan (*V.* Josephine van Brero x *V. dearei*), the first of its type, rekindled the interest in orchids in Singapore and Malaysia after World War II when it won a First Class Certificate from the Royal Horticultural Society.

RIGHT: Vanda John Ede represents the contemporary JVB-type made with rounder *Vanda*.

ABOVE: Ascocenda Bangkok Gold shows the strong influence of *V.* Josephine van Brero.

ABOVE: Vanda Tan Hoon Siang (*V.* Josephine van Brero and *V.* Somsri Pink), an improved JVB-type resulting from the use of a modern strap-leaf *Vanda*.

THE LARGE *VANDAS*

Contemporary round, flat, colourful *Vandas* carry the genes of two species, *Vanda sanderiana* from the Philippines and *Vanda coerulea* from Thailand and Myanmar. They are the results of decades of careful, well-considered breeding by growers in Hawaii, then Thailand, and now also in Florida. Their set back is infrequent flowering: to render them free-flowering the blood of *Ascocentrum curvifolium* is frequently added.

ABOVE: Floral tessellations in hybrids are a mark of *Vanda coerulea* or *V. sanderiana.*

RIGHT: Vanda Sansui Blue; from a simplistic viewpoint, an improved *V. coerulea.* Its inflorescence is carried well above the tip of the plant, a characteristic inherited from *V. coerulea.* Here, the orchid plant dangles from a *Podocarpus* tree growing very close to the author's house and the spray similarly extends downwards in search of light.

ABOVE: Vanda lindenii has been newly re-introduced into Singapore. It shows promise for a new colour range; not pure yellow but interesting.

RIGHT: Vanda lamellata. This hardy species can produce several inflorescences with many flowers, somewhat lacking in brilliance. The free flowering quality possibly decided its selection to produce the very first Aranda, the *Aranda* Deborah. The hybrid flowered in 1938 and was named after Holttum's daughter. It is extremely prolific: a metre tall plant could produce up to a dozen sprays of flowers simultaneously, and afterwards yield numerous axillary offshoots without artificial stimulus like top-cutting. It was a popular up to the mid sixties.

ABOVE & RIGHT: Vanda tessellata is an extremely fragrant Sri Lankan-Indian *Vanda* available in many colours and shapes that open multiple possibilities for breeders. However, its grayish mask is difficult to overcome. Thai breeders have line bred the species to produce improved types.

FOXTAIL ORCHID

ABOVE: Rhynchostylis gigantea was collected once on a fallen branch during a collection expedition in Singapore, but it is unlikely that this species grows naturally so far south. Rapee Sagarik bred a dark purple strain, whose colour is solid when the plant flowers in northern Thailand, but the tepals show a colour break in Bangkok. It is impossible to obtain solid purple flowers without resorting to a cool house in Singapore. A beautiful *alba* form is also available. The common variety is illustrated.

RIGHT: Rhynchostylis retusa, the Foxtail Orchid. Modern line-bred clones in Thailand carry long sprays with sparkling, well arranged flowers. A spell of dry weather is essential for flowering.

THE INFLUENCE OF *RHYNCHOSTYLIS*

Breeding *Ascocenda (Vanda x Ascocentrum)* to *Rhynchostylis* lengthens the raceme and increases the number of flowers. In the manner of *Rhynchostylis*, the flowers of the new trigeneric genus, *Vascostylis* are closely arranged but individual flowers are well displayed and enhanced by a clear delicate pink or purplish tint devoid of any trace of tessellations. *Rhy. coelestis* is usually the preferred species for breeding to *Ascocenda* or *Vanda* because of its long, upright flower spike. These strap-leafed, vandaceous orchids prefer dappled to intense sunlight and are popularly grown tied to trees at a man's height or slightly higher.

ABOVE & RIGHT: Vascostylis Pine Rivers (*Ascda*. Peggy Foo x *Rhy*. coelestis). This is a tetraploid clone which carries four genomes (or four sets of chromosomes). When a tetraploid is bred to a normal diploid plant the resultant triploid is generally free-flowering. But triploids are sterile, so it would be a one-off mating that denies the prospect of continuity.

ABOVE: Renantanda Genting Gem. *RIGHT: Ascocenda* Red Gem

AN EYE FOR RED

Several *Renanthera* and their hybrids (*Aranthera, Renanopsis, Renantanda, Kagawaara*, etc.) and *Ascocentrum curvifolium* hybrids are good sources of red orchids. Many are free flowering, with the *Ascocenda* overcoming the reluctance of strap leaf *Vanda* to flower.

ABOVE: Ascocenda Peggy Foo x *Vanda* Gordon Dillion. This is just one of many beautiful hybrids descended from *Ascda*. Peggy Foo which was bred by Roy Fukumura of Hawaii.

ABOVE: Ascocenda Laksi usually produces several inflorescences simultaneously on a well grown plant although this is not evident in the picture.

SCARLET EYE-CATCHERS: THE *RENANTHERA*

Singapore and Peninsular Malaysia are not the native home of the spectacular *Renanthera* but many beautiful *Renanthera* hybrids originate from this region. Only two species of *Renanthera* are present in Peninsular Malaysia (*R. elongata* near the coast and *R. matutina* in the highlands of the Main Range). *R. elongata* was discovered on Pulau Tekong by Goodenough in 1891.

RIGHT: Renanthera Kalsom is a handsome, red, sun-loving, free flowering orchid that would be a welcome sight in any tropical garden. Bred by Singapore's top orchid hybridizer, Syed Yusof Alsagoff, it ranks among the most successful hybrids ever made in Singapore. The plant is robust, flowers continuously, and the flowers show no premature fading, once a problem plaguing *Renanthera* and its hybrids. Selected clones of *R.* Kalsom have very thick sepals with heavy substance.

ABOVE: Renanthera Singapore Botanic Gardens (*Ren.* Kalsom x *Ren. bella*) The spots in this hybrid are accentuated by those of the newly discovered, North Bornean montane species, *Ren. bella.* It marks a new direction for breeding *Renanthera*.

ABOVE: Renanathera Akihito is named for the Emperor of Japan. Another hybrid of the Singapore Botanic Gardens is *Renantanda* Akihito (*Vanda manila* x *Ren. coccinea*) which was named by the Director of the Botanic Gardens in Penang, Cheang Kok Choy, in 1970.

Two compact *Renanthera* species with different colour prospects to challenge the hybridizer:

ABOVE: Renanthera citrina newly discovered from southern China and Vietnam.

RIGHT: Renanthera monachica, an old friend.

PAGES 92 & 93: Renanthera makes a fantastic backdrop. Singapore Orchid Festival, 2003

POLYPLOIDY MAKES ALL THE DIFFERENCE

ABOVE: Renantanda Prince Norodom Sihanouk was raised by the Singapore Botanic Gardens in 1962, a cross between the salmon coloured *V.* Tan Chay Yan and a hexaploid, red *Renanthera coccinea.* It had red flowers being dominated by the red of the hexaploid parent. Recently, a repeat cross made with a diploid clone of *Ren. coccinea* showed a dominance of *V.* Tan Chay Yan with salmon pink flowers.

RIGHT: An unnamed *Paravanda* made with *Paraphaelnopsis laycockii.* Generally *Pps. laycockii* produces beautiful hybrids but unfortunately the flower stems tend to be short and the flowers are not long lasting, traits that breeders seek to overcome by crossing with a dominant parent possessing contrasting characteristics.

PARAPHALAENOPSIS: A SINGAPOREAN FAVOURITE

Paraphalaenopsis are a group of terete-leaf, epiphytic, monopodial orchids with extremely short stems that were, till fairly recently, known as the *rat-tailed Phalaenopsis*. They are endemic in Borneo and grow high above the ground, attached to tall timber trees. Three species have long been used for breeding to other monopodial orchids in Singapore and Malaysia and eight multigeneric hybrids were named for Singaporean and Malaysian orchid celebrities. A recent nomenclature revision wiped out the list, but the curious looking plants with colourful, two toned flowers remain. Hybrids with *Paraphalaenopsis denevei* and *Paraphalaenopsis serpentilingua* possess a contrasting dark red lip. Hybrids of *Pph. lacycockii* have pink or white tepals.

ABOVE: Paravanda Nelson Mandela is a VIP orchid raised by the Singapore Botanic Gardens named to commemorate the visit of the South African statesman.

RIGHT: Paraphalaenopsis labukensis is a recent discovery which came to light as a result of logging in Borneo (Kalimantan). While the three earlier species are now rare, *Pph. labukensis* is plentiful. It imparts a strong coloration to its hybrids, the *Paravanda* Nelson Mandela being one such example. The lip is white with brown spots, not solid red.

SENTIMENTALITY VS. AUTHORITY

When a hybrid orchid genus is consitituted by three or more genera, the Rules of the International Orchid Commission permit the introduction of a new, independent generic name for the artificial genus that generally ends with the letters '*ara*'. Following the creation of *Holttumara* in 1957, *Ridleyara* in 1962 and *Burkhillara* in 1967 which honour three previous Directors of the Singapore Botanic Gardens, Singapore breeders have managed to register 21 such complex, inter-generic hybrids that include: *Sappanara* (1965), *Laycockara* (1966), *Yapara* (1966), *Teohara* (1967), *Mokara* (1969), *Yusofara* (1972), *Leeara* (1972), *Stamariaara* (1974), *Bokchoonara* (1976), *Edeara* (1976), *Ngara* (91978), *Lauara* (1982), *Pehara* (1982), *Andrewara* (1983), *Alphonsoara* (1988), *Yeepengara* (1997), *Waironara* (1997), *Wailaiara* (1998), *Chuatianara* (2000), *Engkianara* (2000) and *Waibengara* (2001). This long list of 24 new genera from the little red dot exceeds that of any other orchid-breeding nation and attests to the vibrant orchid scene in Singapore.

The names carry a sentimental value for their originators and they generally commemorate the luminaries of the local orchid scene.

In January 2003, sometime after the designation of a separate generic status for *Paraphalaenopsis* (which was formerly included in *Phalaenopsis* but well known as the rat-tail type) the International Orchid Registrar announced that new generic names have been assigned to nine of the complex genera that included *Paraphalaenopsi*s in their make-up. The opinion of the creators of the first hybrids of these genera was not sought, nor their agreement with the change, or whether they had an alternative name in mind, and despite the fact that one was recently published in the 21st century. The new names carry no association with Singapore. This naturally caused consternation in Singapore which is the centre for most breeding activity involving *Paraphalaenopsis*. Petitions were swept aside.

This page regrets the demise of the eight names *(Bokchoonara, Edeara, Laycockara, Sappanara, Stamariaara,Waibengara, Yapara* and *Yeepengara)* which included some that commemorate people who were pioneers of hybridization and promoters of orchids in this part of the world: John Laycock, founder president of the Malayan Orchid Society, Dr. Yeoh Bok

Choon, past president of the Malayan Orchid Society, John Ede who ran the magnificent Singapore Orchids for several decades, Bajuri bin Sappan the friendly collector and breeder for the Singapore Botanic Gardens. As orchid growers in these parts still cherish these names you will see them written on the labels in many gardens.

BELOW: Bokchoonara Khaw Bian Huat is a combination of *Arachnis, Paraphalaenopsis, Ascocentrum* and *Vanda.*

DENDROBIUM

Everyone in Singapore is familiar with this orchid, but perhaps not with the fact that *Dendrobium* species which are native to Singapore and Malaysia are all very modest. We made our hybrids with imported species. Singapore sits at the edge of the geographic distribution of this outstanding genus, and from the early days Singapore growers were able to collect species and hybrids of horticultural value from Indonesia, Papua New Guinea and the Philippines. Breeding with *Dendrobium* commenced in Singapore in 1933, and the first hybrid (*D.* Constance bred by John Laycock) did not flower until 1941. To-day breeders expect to see their hybrids flowering within three years of pollination. Over the period 1933–2003, 551 *Dendrobium* hybrids raised in Singapore were registered.

RIGHT: Dendrobium cut flowers at the Singapore Orchid Show, 2007

SHAPES AND FORM

The science of taxonomy is all about similarities and differences in species. Orchid collectors share the same fascination. The new breed of young orchid enthusiasts prefer to grow unusual species plants than the near-perfect hybrids because the latter are now commonplace, due to mericloning. In the following pages, we shall, now and then, take a look at some novel species.

ABOVE: Dendrobium lowii is endemic in Borneo. Its golden yellow flowers last for a month.

RIGHT: Denrobium dearei. This is a popular lowland species from Borneo and the Phillippines commonly grown for its beautiful, pure white, long-lasting fragrant flowers

PAGE 106: Dendrobium bracteosum is a popular cultivated variety.

PAGE 107: Dendrobium unicum is a deciduous species from Northern Thailand.

SHAPES OR FORM

Horticulturists are aware that variations in the shape, colour, texture and height of the plants in a garden are essential considerations when trying to add interest in a garden. One does not have such luxury with orchids unless one is prepared to grow a big range of genera, but orchid flowers do come in a wide range of shapes as shown in the next few pages.

BELOW: Dendrobium floresianum occurs in Flores and Nusa Tenggara, Indonesia.

A Dendrobium species from the Section *Calcarifera* from the Indonesian island of Flores.

RIGHT: Dendrobium macrophyllum is a native of East Indonesia and Papua New Guinea. It belongs to a neglected section of *Dendrobium* called *Latourea* which is now receiving attention from hybridizers.

THE RARE OR EXOTIC SPECIES

Many people enjoy seeing a rare or exotic species. The best place to look for rare or unusual orchids is at a Show organized by an Orchid Society. The Orchid Society of South East Asia (OSSEA) has a mini-show of plants belonging to members at its monthly meetings held on the first Sunday of the month at the Singapore Botanic Gardens.

ABOVE: Inobulbum (Dendrobium) munificum an unusual *'Dendrobium'* with large, fat pseudobulbs and thick, fleshy leaves 30 cm x 4 cm is now raised to a separate genus. The inflorescences are arching, up to 30 cm long with many (up to 200) closely arranged, olive green or yellow flowers of heavy substance. The tepals are overlaid with brown and the lip is streaked with red. The flowers open in the morning and close at night. The species is restricted to the southern mountains of New Caledonia at 200–700 metres.

RIGHT: Dendrobium panduriferum is a lowland epiphyte distributed from Myanmar, across Peninsular Thailand and Malaysia to Kalimantan. In the Malay Peninsula it is uncommon and found only in Perak and Pahang, occurring in the lowlands and peat swamps. The pseudobulbs are slender, up to 60 cm long, with thin leaves. A dozen greenish yellow or olive brown flowers with tepals overlaid with crimson veins are carried on a short inflorescence on leafless stems.

UNUSUAL FINDS

ABOVE: Dendrobium Adora Nishii is not the common florist orchid but a rare primary hybrid between *Den. alexandrae* (only rediscovered in 1995 after a lapse of 90 years) and *Den. spectabile,* two members of the *Spectabile* Alliance whose flowers have the most bizarre appearance. The result: more of the same! The 40 cm inflorescence carries many well-spaced, yellow flowers possessing narrow, twisted petals with undulating border and a long twisted, pointed tongue with prominent brownish veins.

RIGHT: Dendrobium jiewhoeii is so new it has yet to be mentioned in the numerous tomes on *Dendrobium.* First discovered by Anthony Lamb at 900 metres on the Crocker Range in Sabah in 2007, it has since been known to also occur in Sarawak. The orchid is named after John Tan Jiew Hoe who is president of the Malayan Nature Society and an expert on begonias. His father, Tan Hoon Siang was a president of the Malayan Orchid Society and the breeder of *Vanda* Tan Chay Yan. John is a strong supporter of the Orchid Society of South East Asia (OSSEA). The flowers of *Den. jiewhoeii* are creamy yellow throughout and they are arranged spirally to face all directions.

LEFT: Dendrobium ionopus is from the hills of northern Luzon. Its flowers last a week to 10 days.

ABOVE: Dendrobium farmeri is a lowland species distributed in Myanmar, peninsular Thailand and the northern states of the Malay Peninsula. It flowers several times a year in Singapore but the 40 delicate pink flowers on the pendent inflorescence only last for a week.

HYBRIDS OF THE *SPATHULATA* (HORN) *DENDROBIUMS*

In this section we shall look at the *horn*, earlier also referred to as *cane*, *Dendrobiums* which are a favourite with commercial growers because the hybrids flower continuously and produce long-lasting flowers that travel well. They exist in a wide range of colours. Most of the species occur in Indonesia or Papua New Guinea with a few in the Philippines and in Queensland, Australia.

LEFT: Dendrobium stratiotes.

ABOVE: Dendrobium Ryzhkoiva x *lasianthera* is an outstanding hybrid raised by the Singapore Botanic Gardens. A superior tetraploid clone has been identified.

ABOVE: Dendrobium lasianthera with its large lip and a double twist in the petals has the further advantage that its flowers last for three months. Andree Millar who rediscovered the plant in 1976 named the various clones under their habitat: Sepik Blue, May River Red, etc.

RIGHT: A so-called intermediate *Dendrobium*, a cross between *D. biggibum (D. phalaenopsis)* and a *Spathulata Dendrobium*. Such hybrids are usually free flowering throughout the year. The flowers are of good substance, nowadays of deep purple, and will last for a month.

21ST CENTURY *DENDROBIUMS*

LEFT: Dendrobium Catherine Jane Tkatchenko (*D.* Masako Taki x *D. lasianthera*) bred by Neo Tuan Hong. Displaying multiple stiff upright inflorescences, with numerous, well arranged, pink flowers with their dark crimson lips that remain at a horizontal level this *Dendrobium* stole the show and was voted Best Plant in the Singapore Orchid Show held in December 2006.

ABOVE: Dendrobium Tan Tock Seng Hospital (*D.* Tan Horns x *D.* Mini Twist), a new hybrid bred by Syed Yusof Alsagoff. The erect inflorescence holds many erect flowers with slim twisted petals in an unusual orange-brown with a contrasting violet lip. One seldom encounters such elegance in an orchid.

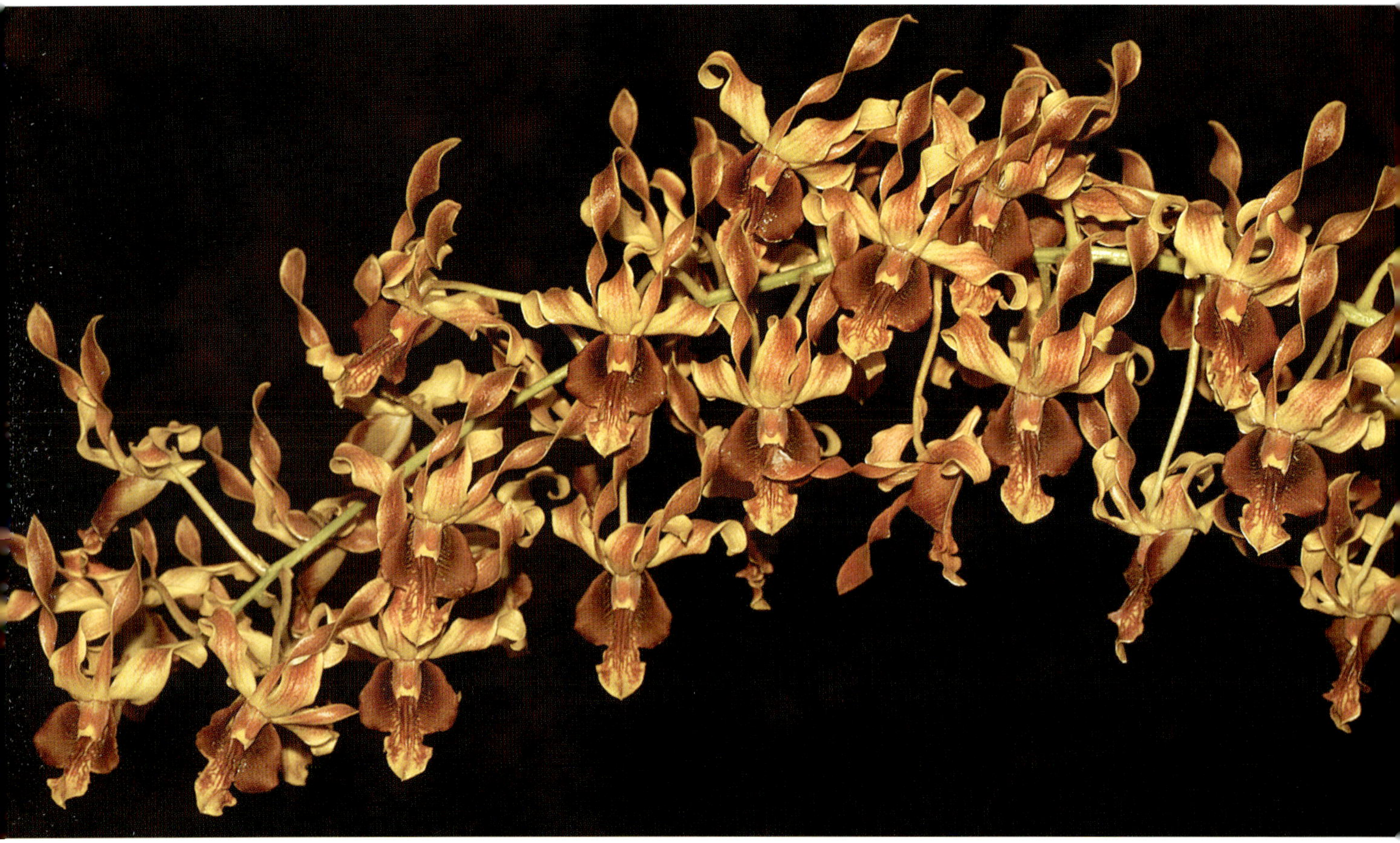

AN OUTSTANDING HORN-TYPE *DENDROBIUM*

Dendrobium Jeffrey Tan is an excellent Malaysian hybrid. It comes in several colours, and three clones received awards at the Singapore Orchid Show in July 2007. The flowers have a nice shape, with erect petals and they do not flop downwards (as many horn-*Dendrobiums* do). The lip is large, the colour is bright, the flowers are of good substance and they are well arranged. Those of the brown clone appear to be a bit too crowded and I much prefer the arrangement of the flowers in the upright red clone. I prefer an upright habit to a horizontal or arching type, one reason being that it needs a stouter rachis to hold the flowers vertically. There are no fixed rules for appreciating horn *Dendrobium*: these are merely some of the qualities that one should look for. Balance is a keyword in judging their form.

ABOVE & RIGHT: Two awarded clones of *Dendrobium* Jeffrey Tan

DOMINANCE

Experience shows that in its first generation (F1) hybrids *Dendrobium discolor* exerts a dominance by producing flowers with highly twisted petals and sepals with undulating margins in many shades of yellow, green and brown. The hybrids are extremely free flowering, producing long sprays with many flowers and a well grown plant will carry many sprays simultaneously. *Dendrobium discolour* and F1, F2 progeny were much employed when Singapore started breeding *Dendrobium*. However, the flowers tended to be crowded, floppy and nodding. *Dendrobium sutiknoi* is a new Indonesian species introduced at the turn of the millennium. Its flowers have the same olive, brownish green colour of *D. discolor* and they are larger but fewer, well spaced, with an erect bearing, and long, narrow twisted petals. When these two species were bred to each other, some of the resulting hybrids had erect inflorescences, and some had arching inflorescences. All the flowers were large, similarly coloured, and they all carried erect petals of greater width than those of *D. sutiknoi*. This hybrid is not an end in itself, but it shows the dominance of *D. sutiknoi* and a new direction is open for breeding *D. discolor*.

LEFT: Dendrobium discolor x D. sutiknoi.

ABOVE: Dendrobium discolor. This is a superlative clone.

NEW DEVELOPMENTS IN *SPATHULATA DENDROBIUM* HYBRIDS

LEFT: An improvement has been made by producing clearer venation in the large *D. taurinum* type lip which greatly enhances the appearance of this hybrid. The lip is accentuated by the halo of white from the proximal portion of the petals and sepals and the colour of their distal half is sufficiently subdued to give a soft look.

ABOVE: Pure white is a very unusual colour in *Spathulata Dendrobium* and this is a worthy avenue of pursuit for the Singapore Botanic Gardens which raised this hybrid.

A V.I.P. ORCHID
DENDROBIUM NAJIB ROSMAH

For the past 50 years, the Singapore Botanic Gardens has commemorated the visits of distinguished visitors to its Gardens with the naming of new orchid hybrids. This *Dendrobium* is the latest. Several V.I.P. Orchids are featured here and there in this volume. They may also be viewed in the National Orchid Garden beside Burkhill House.

LEFT & ABOVE: Dendrobium Najib Rosmah, two distinct clones. *Dendrobium* Najib Rosmah is named after the Prime Minister of Malaysia and his wife. This exceptional hybrid comes in different colours, white and olive green with a contrasting purple lip, white overlaid with purple stripes, a contrasting purple lip and twisted petals in a striking orange-brown, and clones with lighter hues. Its heavy substance is remarkable.

TWO ADDITIONAL V.I.P. *DENDROBIUMS*

ABOVE: Dendrobium Elizabeth was named for Her Majesty Queen Elizabeth II of the United Kingdom when she visited the Singapore Botanic Gardens in 1972. The hybrid originated from the Singapore Botanic Gardens and the parent plant *D.* Noor Aishah had been named for the first First Lady of Singapore, wife of President Yusof Ishak. *D.* Noor Aishah has produced quite a handful of V.I.P. Orchids which include *D.* Michiko, *D.* Tien Soeharto, *D.* Rahah, *D.* Curazon Aquino, and *D.* Mie Fukuda. The absence of *D. schulleri* in their ancestry is noteworthy.

RIGHT: Dendrobium Margaret Thatcher (*D.* Concham x *D. lasianthera*) was named by the Singapore Botanic Gardens for Mrs. Margaret Thatcher when she visited Singapore in 1986. The rigid, spiraling red petals and the general boldness of the flowers are so appropriate for this Iron Lady who kept a firm hand on Britain during her two terms as Prime Minister. The hybrid was originated by the Singapore Botanic Gardens, a product of its own line breeding. The spiraling petals came from the *D. lasianthera* and *D. discolor* (syn. *D. undulatum*) in its parentage.

ABOVE: Dendrobium Masahito and Hanako This is another V.I.P. orchid which was named for their Imperial Highnesses, Prince and Princess Hitachi of Japan in 2000. It is unique for an orchid to be named after two persons, but it so happens that the Rules of Registration allows for three words. The delicate powder pink overlaid on ivory in the coloration of the flowers has an exquisite match.

RIGHT: Dendrobium Sianne Velvet x *nindii*. This outstanding *Dendrobium* bears long sprays of well arranged purplish flowers with dark broad lips. The characteristics of this plant are dominated by *Dendrobium nindii* (*D. ionoglossum*) which is prevalent in Papua New Guinea but considered threatened in Australia due to habitat destruction in the latter locale. *D. nindii* is taller than a man, with canes that are so stout they look like sugar cane. It bears many sprays with numerous purple flowers towards the end of these stems and its flowering is not seasonal.

INTERMEDIATE *DENDROBIUMS* FOR LANDSCAPING

The so-called *Intermediate Dendrobiums* are hybrids between *Dendrobium biggibum* (syn. *D. phalaenopsis*) and the *Spathulata Dendrobiums.* They have a rounder shape than the horn types and they flower abundantly throughout the year. They form the backbone of the florist industry. The plants are about 60 cm tall and are excellent for landscapes and indoor decoration.

LEFT & ABOVE: White *Intermediate Dendrobium* in a landscape at the National Orchid Garden. Many varieties of *Dendrobium* in a range of colours are arranged in landscapes in the Garden.

Whenever I see *Dendrobium phalaenopsis* many stories come to mind. First, among the many telegrams and letters that Wilhelm Micholitz (active 1887–1914) sent to his boss David Sander when he was recuperating in between missions in Singapore, was one describing the discovery of *Dendrobium schroderianum* (syn. *D. biggibum, D. phalaenopsis*). The two to three thousand plants which he had collected in New Guinea would be worth a fortune when they arrived in London, so there was much excitement. Unfortunately, the the plants was destroyed when the ship transporting them caught fire in the Celebes. The telegram read: *Ship Burnt. What do Micholitz*. Sander shot a reply: *Return. Recollect.* Micholitz responded: *Too Late. Rainy Season.* Sander insisted: *Return Sander.*

In the spring of 1891 (autumn down-under), Micholitz discovered a new colony of "the Denrobe (sic). They had just finished growing and were in full bloom and oh what a glorious thing it is. I forgot my troubles when I saw the first on some rocks in the little village where I was staying, and where they grow on bare limestone between a great number of human skulls and bones. …"*

In the event, one plant arrived in England still attached to a skull, causing a sensation when it was put for auction. The *Dendrobiums* fetched several thousand guineas, but in his correspondence, Micholitz had to repeatedly beg Sander to renew his credit. Agricultural and horticultural workers on the ground seldom receive their just reward.

* Ref: Swinson A (1970): *Frederick Sander: The Orchid King.* London: Hodder & Stoughton.

CLONING OR MERISTEM PROPAGATION

Meristem tissue culture has been employed to produce large numbers of cloned orchids for the cut-flower trade and to a limited extent to make prized plants available to the average hobbyist. Because growth regulators are employed in great excess of their pysiological concentration, the process does not always produce true clones. Mutations (alterations to the genes) do occur;some are lost,others duplicated, and entire sets of chromosomes may be replicated. Sometimes these produce interesting

colour forms, pelorism (petals aquiring the shape of their lips) or larger, rounder, firmer flowers due to polyploidy (an increase in the sets of chromosomes). It is always interesting to walk through a field of mericlone plants, even if one is not always certain of encountering a desirable mutation.

LEFT & ABOVE: Colour variation in *Denodrobium* resulting from meristem propagation (cloning).

The Moth Orchid
Phalaenopsis

RIGHT: A magnificent artistic display of *Phalaenopsis* was put up by the National Orchid Garden in February 2009. Several rare species were also included in the display.

PAGES 142 & 143: White *Phalaenopsis*

THE STARS OF SARAWAK

Phalaenopsis bellina is popular in this part of the world because it is pretty, fragrant, free flowering and does not require much care being seemingly free of pest and disease, unlike the showy, large *Phalaenopsis* which are prone to rot during the rainy season if they are not properly sheltered. It is endemic in Borneo and nearly all the plants have come through Kuching. In Sarawak it is known as *Bunga Low*, (Low's blossom), after the Scottish naturalist who came to Southeast Asia on a collecting expedition at the age of 20 and rose to be one of the most successful British administrators during the colonial period. Sir Hugh Low (1824–1905) was the Colonial Secretary in Borneo from 1948 to 1850, and the British Resident of Perak (in Peninsular Malaysia) from 1977-1899. He has numerous plants and animals named after him, including *Cymbidium lowii, Dendrobium lowii, Dimorphis lowii* and *Paphiopedilum lowii.*

P. bellina used to abundant on the branches of the illipe nut, *Shorea gysbertsiana* growing near river banks south of Lundu in western Sarawak. Since both the illipe nut and the orchid were valuable commercial crops, they were simultaneously harvested. Dayak maidens sported the flower on their left ear during longhouse parties. By 1961, the orchid was greatly endangered. John Seal who was familiar with the area spent a day looking for the orchid in its natural habitat without finding any. However, it was still abundant in Indonesian Borneo (Kalimantan). Flowers of the wild plants tend to be bow legged, but line bred flowers are star shaped with broad petals and sepals. The white form is rare.

P. bellina was formerly called *P. violacea*, Sarawak strain, and for the reader's interest we illustrate the so-called Sumatran strain here, so that all three strains of the former *P. violacea* are illustrated.

ABOVE: Phalaenopsis bellina var. *alba*

LEFT: The new, Sumatran strain of *P. violacea.* The sepals and petals are narrower, thus accentuating its star shape. The petals have an upward tilt rather like the almond-shaped oriental eyes and the inflorescence is long.

THE STARS OF SARAWAK: *PHALAENOPSIS GIGANTEA*

Phalaenopsis gigantea has the largest leaves among orchids, these reaching up to 1.5 x 0.8 metres, an even sheet of grayish green, smooth textured but of heavy substance. Most times, one only admires the plant because one must look behind the leaves to see the striking, red spotted, round flowers which open simultaneously on the hanging inflorescence. That would be extremely difficult to do in nature, considering that this species grows in primary forests, on the branches of iron wood trees (*Eusiderosylon zwageri*), often more than 25 metres above the ground. Once common in Tawau, logging has endangered the species, but nursery bred plants and hybrids are readily available, the latter often spectacular, and in the author's opinion, a much better bet for the average grower.

ABOVE: Phalaenopsis Teoh Tee Teong *x bellina* bred by Law Moi Hwa. This cross has 87.5 per cent *P. bellina* and 12.5 per cent *P. gigantea*, just enough of the latter to produce a rounder form while essentially retaining the form, colour and behaviour of the desired *P. bellina*.

RIGHT: Hybrid of *Phalaenopsis gigantea* with similar vegetative but a different flower form.

ABOVE: White *Doritaenopsis*. Many so-called *Phalaenopsis* on the market today are *Doritaenopsis* and not pure *Phalaenopsis*. The advantages are vigour, resilience and floriferousness.

ABOVE: Doritaenopsis with novel colouration. Charles L. Beard of West Palm Beach who started back-crossing to *Phalaenopsis* in the late sixties introduced bicolours, but not such unique coloration.

PAGES 152 & 153: Doritaenopsis Leopard Prince.

SOURCES OF YELLOW AND RED IN NOVELTY *PHALENOPSIS*

Two species which contribute to the new colours in novelty *Phalaenopsis* are *Phalaenopsis amboinensis* and *Phalaenopsis venosa*.

LEFT: Phalaenopsis amboinensis.

ABOVE: Phalaenopsis venosa.

NOVELTY *PHALAENOPSIS*

Orchid fanciers sometimes shun the large many flowered *Phalaenopsis* and prefer to collect the small flowered simpler hybrids which display an interesting range of colours. Whereas form cannot be ignored, the emphasis here is on clear, brilliant colours and distinct spots or bars. There are usually not many flowers on an inflorescence, but a strong plant particularly those with *P. amboinensis* in its background may carry several inflorescences simultaneously.

ABOVE: Phalaenopsis David Lim (*P. amboinensis x P. gigantea*).

RIGHT: Phalaenopsis Dou-dii Pride. Phalaenopsis of such superb form, size and colour leaves only number of blooms and their arrangement as features still to be improved. Connoisseurs never stop asking for more.

Standards of Excellence

The criteria set by horticultural organizations for excellence in flowers, inclusive of orchids, call for: fullness or roundness; flat form; larger than average size; bright clear colours; distinct markings, if these are present; heavy substance; good arrangement of the flowers; showy display, preferably above or away from the vegetative portion of the plant; and long lasting qualities. These are not the requirements of insect pollinators which are generally attracted by scent, pheromones, mimicry, tactile stimuli, sexual gratification, and nectar. Single day wonders that bloom gregariously, like the Pigeon Orchid, survive very well in nature. Natural and artificial selection thus do not go hand in hand, and this is one of the problems confronting the ex-situ conservation of orchid species. Human pollinators tend to favour plants that they find attractive and eventually they end up with a prized collection of orchid species which are quite different from the average plant collected in the wild. Once, when I requested the famous Singapore taxonomist, Peter O'Byrne to help me decide whether a flower was really *Rhynchostylis retusa* or a hybrid, he told me that the species has been so line-bred that contemporary forms may be quite distinct from one another and from the wild species.

ABOVE: Phalaenopsis violacea, Perak variety. It has an open form but is already line-bred and selected.

ABOVE: Phalaenopsis Penang Ruby bred by Michael Ooi displays the trend towards roundness that hybridizers strive to achieve when breeding with *P. violacea* and *P. bellina.*

Oriental vs. Occidental Standards

Oriental taste and criteria for judging beauty differ considerably from western ideals. In the past, Chinese *Cymbidiums* were admired for the elegance of their foliage, the fragrance, grace, simplicity and refinement of the flowers, an air of nobility that eschews boldness or a garish appearance. Tokugawa nobility in ancient Japan shared such values and their admiration for *Neofinetia falcata* provides a glimpse of their concept of quality. However, globalization during the past 50 years have swept away many oriental values, in food, culture, religion, architecture, and even in orchids. There are now several volumes dedicated to the cataloging, description and promotion of a wide range of Chinese peloric *Cymbidium*, and some of these clones are monstrosities that are far removed from the refinement and nobility their ancestors, although one could say, from my western tinted viewpoint, that a few are reasonably attractive. Orchid societies in Asia are striving to re-introduce eastern standards for judging *Cymbidium*, and to judge scents in orchids, but they are fighting uphill battles.

ABOVE: Paravandrum Sze Chian Fai bred by Law Moi Hwa won the World Orchid Conference Trust Trophy for innovative hybridizing in Singapore in 2008.

RIGHT: Dendrobium spectabile. One has to get into the mind of an insect to find this beautiful.

ABOVE: Malaxis metallica is a curious botanical from Borneo with leaves of purple and a metallic lustre.

ABOVE: Malaxis elegans (syn. *Microstylis elegans*) is a rare, geophytic species from Sarawak.

ABOVE: Ludisia discolor, a jewel orchid.

RIGHT: Habenaria medusae. Habenaria is the largest genus of geophytic orchids with some 600 members found in areas with distinct wet and dry seasons. The plant needs a dormant phase to flower properly, even just to survive. The genus is distinguished by a large expanse of a lip that is flat, multi-lobulated and monochromatic, but few lips are as unique as this one.

Orchids in the Coolhouse

Many attractive tropical orchids are found at high elevations and quite a number of lowland orchid species are stimulated to bloom at temperatures below 20 degrees Centigrade. If they are placed in a coolhouse at blooming time the plants will have more flowers, larger, flat flowers with broader sepals and petals and an overall improved shape. The flowers have better substance, their texture is finer and they last longer. Thus it makes sense to have a coolhouse in the tropics. This is exactly what the Singapore Botanic Gardens and some commercial growers have done. Presently cost and space makes it still prohibitive for the hobbyist. In the next few pages, some orchids in the Coolhouse of the National Orchid Garden will be shown, and others that would do well in one.

BELOW: Dendrochilum latifolium var. *micranthum* is found in the Philippines above 1,200 metres.

RIGHT: Dendrochilum longifolia in the Coolhouse of the National Orchid Garden, Singapore. It is distributed in Indonesia, Malaysia, the Philippines and Papua New Guinea, occuring between 600 to 2200 metres above sea level.

ABOVE: Dendrochilum gracile is another common regional species with many flowers.

RIGHT: Coelogyne swaniana makes a spectacular sight with its long inflorescence of flowers which open together. It grows attached to artificial rock and is often in bloom.

THE PLEBIAN AND THE EXOTIC

Only a collector of *Paphiopedilum* would respond differently to these two species of the Lady Slipper Orchids and value them disproportionately.

ABOVE: Paphiopedilum lowii is almost perpetually in bloom at the Coolhouse, usually carrying three to five (up to seven) flowers on a long inflorescence. Discovered in 1846, this spectacular orchid is widespread in Indonesia and Malaysia at 250–1,600 metres and unlike most *Paphiopedilums,* as an epiphyte. It is closely related to the Philippine *P. haynaldianum* which carries prominent spots on its dorsal sepal. An *alba* form of *P. lowii* has been discovered in Sarawak.

RIGHT: Paphiopedilum sugiyamamum is so recent, it is not even mentioned in many learned monographs on the *Paphiopedilum*. Many new *Paphs* were described in the past 60 years and more new species possibly await discovery.

ORCHIDS WORTH A KING'S RANSOM

LEFT: Paphiopedilum sanderianum.

ABOVE: Paphiopedilum rothschildianum.

Paul Koopowitz (1982) recalled how efforts to re-establish the rare *Paphiopedilum* went up in a blaze of vengeance set by loggers when an attempt was made to extend the Kinabalu Nature Reserve.

LEFT: Paphiopedilum micranthum is one of a handful of Chinese *Paphiopedilums* that amazed the western orchid world when they were announced in the early 1980s. The members of this subgenus *(Parvisepalum)* are characterized by a large, globular, thin textured pouch. The semicircular petals are an additional attractive feature of *P. micrantum.*

ABOVE: Paphiopedilum Magic Lantern has inherited the good qualities of *P. micranthum*

WHY DO PEOPLE CLIMB MOUNTAINS?

The passion to cultivate the difficult and the rare (*top left: Paphiopedilum* Ho Chi Minh; *bottom left: P.* In Cham White) rather than the easy species (*above: P. godfroyae*) share similar roots. The hybrid *Paphiopedilums* on the left are derived from montane Chinese-Vietnamese species and they require cool surroundings, whereas *P. godfroyae* is found near sea level in Peninsular Thailand and it has no special requirements in Singapore, except perhaps limestone.

MORE COOLHOUSE ORCHIDS

Two very uncommon orchids that are not found anywhere else in Singapore except in the Coolhouse are these two *Robiquetia* which are monopodial orchids native to the region that extends from the Philippines and Indonesia to Australia and the Pacific Islands. There are about 40 species in the genus with only one in Malaysia. The droopy inflorescence carries many flowers which face all directions. Flowers on these two inflorescences never fully open.

To get a glimpse of orchids from the temperate countries, always remember to visit the Singapore Orchid Show and look for the group exhibits by the Orchid Societies of Australia, China, Japan and the United Kingdom.

ABOVE: Group Exhibit by the Orchid Society of Great Britain, 2007 Singapore Orchid Show

RIGHT: Lycaste in a Group Exhibit by the Japan Orchid Society, 2007 Singapore Orchid Show

Fragrance in Orchids

Vanda tessellata is native to Sri Lanka and the southern tip of the Indian Peninsula. There are several colour forms but the common quality it imparts to all its hybrids is a strong fragrance, quite unlike that of other garden flowers. However, the very intense scent varies with the variety of *V. tessellata*. According to Roman Kaiser, an authority on perfumes, the scent of the grey-green brown coloured flower (used in breeding *V.* Mimi Palmer) is based on linalool, methyl benzoate, cinnamic aldehyde and methyl cinnamate with minute amounts of benzyl acetate, alpha-ionone, 3-phenylpropanal, p-cresol and indole. Other clones have (E) ocimene in combination with other compounds.

ABOVE: Vanda Mimi Palmer, a cross between *V.* Tan Chay Yan and *V. tessellata* is fragrant and so are its hybrids like *V.* Overseas Union Bank.

RIGHT: An extremely fragrant, line-bred strain of *V. tessellata* raised in Thailand.

MORE ORCHIDS WITH FRAGRANCE

LEFT: Vanda Overseas Union Bank has *V. tessellata* only once in its make-up, but it retains the strong fragrance of this grandparent. The *V. dearei* three generations back may also have contributed to its fragrance.

ABOVE: Vanda denisoniana was promoted by Rapee Sagarik as a source of concolour yellow in *Vanda*. It also has a lovely fragrance. Thai hybridizers started using the species for their crosses only after they had produced an improved clone by inter-clonal breeding. The wild species is protected by law in Thailand. About 400 hybrids now contain *V. denisoniana* in their make-up and in some the yellow colour is masked. *Vanda dearei* and *V. denisoniana* both contribute to the clear yellow colour of *Mokara* Zaleha Alsagoff which has the only First Class Certificate from the Orchid Society of South East Asia.

ORCHIDS ARE MOST FRAGRANT IN THE MORNING

The fragrance of these two orchids is strongest in the morning and I have many plants growing outside my kitchen. *Phalaenopsis bellina* has a rosy-floral scent based on linalool, citronellol, nerol and geraniol, while the scent of its sister species, the Perak *P. violacea* is overlaid with cinnamic from the presence of cinnamic alcohol, cinnayl acetate and cinnamic aldehyde.

ABOVE: Phalaenopsis bellina, formerly known as the Bornean variety of *P. violacea*

RIGHT: Dendrobium anosmum, a common lowland species in Malaysia, Indonesia and Thailand. Unlike other soft-cane *Dendrobium* which are generally seasonal, *D. anosmum* flowers several times a year and it is well worth growing. There is also a beautiful *alba* variety.

DAUGHTERS OF THE AIR *(AERIDES)*

Aerides was named by a Portuguese missionary in 1790 who was fascinated by their epiphytic nature. They are seasonal bloomers and remain in bloom for only two weeks but during that time they fill their ambience with a strong floral fragrance. Among the 18 member species, the common Thai-Malaysian species *A. odorata*, as its name implies, is the most strongly scented. However, these days it is not so commonly grown because it is not as attractive as the Philippine *A. lawrenceae*

ABOVE: Aerides lawrenceae produces a rosy floral scent described as 'sweet, honey-like' due to a high content of methyl phenylacetate and 'fresh' because of neral, geranial and farnesal.

RIGHT: Aerides Edward, a spectacular, colourful hybrid raised by the Singapore Botanic Gardens.

THE BAD GUYS

For optimal survival, it is essential that orchid species do not compete for the same pollinators. Those that prefer to be pollinated by flies or midges release the scent of algae, yeast, crustacean, or rotting meat. The most notorious orchid is the *Bulbophyllum beccarii* which emits the stench of carrion. It is said that when this orchid was accidentally allowed to flower in the confines of a glass house at Kew, the premises was rapidly emptied of its visitors.

ABOVE: Liparis viridifolia. This common lowland Malesian orchid is pollinated by flies and midges. Its flowers give off the scent of algae and crustacean. Additionally, they release two pleromones identical to those produced by female workers of *Paravespula vulgaris.*

RIGHT: Bulbophyllum beccarii is not an orchid that one would see on display, but in the forest, it can be found by following its smell when it is in bloom. Blue bottle flies are attracted to this malodorous orchid. This photograph was taken in a coolhouse. Later in the day, when exhibited outdoors, it was covered with flies.

Oddities

Renathrella histrionica is a odd little epiphytic orchid which prefers mangrove to trees growing on solid ground. But it is only one of about seven species also inhabiting the mangroves of Peninsular Malaysia and Singapore (the others being *Bulbophyllum concinnum, Bulbophyllum blumei, Cymbidium finlaysonianum, Liparis gibbosa, Renanthera elongata,* and *Thelasis pygmaea.*) In far off Florida collectors are haunted by the image of the forbidden, beautiful, wiry, white Ghost Orchid, *Polyrrhiza lindenii* which grows only in Fakahatchee swamp. Now, the Ghost Orchid may not be collected from the wild but nobody had thought about growing this orchid before the conservation laws came into effect. *Renanthrella histrionica* is not endangered because it is nowhere as beautiful, its small, yellow flowers bordered with red at the edges of the segments being upside down, and opening only one or two at a time on a progressively extending inflorescence.

Southeast Asia is also home to another oddity, leafless orchids like *Taeniophyllum* and *Chilochista.* whose leaves are reduced to tiny scales while their green roots take on the job of photosynthesis. By necessity these are small plants.

BELOW: Renanthrella histrionica.

RIGHT: Chilochista lunifera or *Phaya Rai Bai* flowers in March and April in northern Thailand.

LEFT: National Orchid Garden display of *Phalaenopsis* in the Tan Hoon Siang Mist House, February 2009. Several rare species were also included in the display.

RIGHT: Singapore Orchid Show, December 2006. A group of strap leaf *Vanda* and other orchids exhibited by the Royal Horticultural Society of Thailand. Various affiliates of the Orchid Society of Southeast Asia support one another's Shows by sending orchid plants in bloom or cut orchids for exhibit at their Shows.

ABOVE: Prizewinning exhibit by the Singapore's Bedok View Secondary School. Many students have an interest in orchids and schools have programmes that allow schoolchildren to make hybrids. They are also encouraged by the Orchid Society of Southeast Asia to participate in its Shows where a section is assigned to the schools.

ABOVE: A beautifully colour-harmonized arrangement of orchids by the Japan Orchid Society at the Singapore Orchid Show, 2008.

LEFT: National Orchid Garden, Singapore, February 2009.

ABOVE: Dendrobium leis from Thailand, Singapore Orchid Show, 2006.

Orchids in the Landscape

Orchids being epiphytes, they are very charming when they are incorporated into the landscape. Large plants like *Grammatophyllum* or *Aerides* species need to be placed in the fork of a tree, but some genera, like *Dendrobium, Phalaenopsis, Bulbophyllum, Ascocenda, Vanda* and *Cattleya* do well when they are tied to the trunk or branches of a tree. Some will even grow on rocks.

LEFT: Grammatophyllum scriptum growing in the crotch of a mature *Cassia fistula* tree. The plant has been growing there for three years and at the last flowering it produced 12 sprays of flowers.

ABOVE: Paraphalaenopsis labukensis tied to a tree fern and attached to a cypress. It is not growing luxuriantly, I suspect, because it is not high enough and the branches of the tree are too fine. *Paraphalaenopsis labukensis* produces rambling roots that travel a great distance.

VANDA ARE EPIPHYTES*

ABOVE & RIGHT: These vandaceous orchids have been returned to their epiphytic state. They are growing on my *Podocarpus* tree. Seeing these flowers from the bedroom window or looking up to them from the ground gives a sense of seeing orchids in their natural environment. This is the way that I prefer to grow orchids, but it is not always practical if one wants to keep many plants that include seedlings of new crosses.

PRECEDING PAGE: Quarter-terete *Vanda* Chao Phraya. Roots of terete *Vanda (Papilionanthe)* usually ramble across the ground or in a swamp searching for nutrients while the stems climb over one another and on tree stumps in search of light. Such orchids and their popular hybrids (terete, quarter-terete, semi-terete, three-quarter terete *Vanda*) make an impressive show as a group in a sunny location.

* *Epiphyte*: from the Greek, *epi* (upon) + *phuton* (plant, tree).
Lithophytes grow on rocks; geophytes are terrestrial.

ONE SPOT OF RED

There is a Chinese saying, attributed to the artist Qi Baishi, that one spot of red suffices to indicate the arrival of spring. These two small orchids do well in a tropical garden.

ABOVE: Liparis latifolia is a colourful epiphyte found in montane, lowland and peat swamp forests in Peninsular Malaysia, Thailand, and Indonesia.

RIGHT: Dendrobium faciferum from Maluku was recently introduced into the National Orchid Garden of Singapore. Scarlet is uncommon in *Dendrobium* and the species is free flowering.

ORCHID NAMES

Orchid names are commonly derived from Greek words which refer to some characteristic of the flowers or the plant, or the name honors a person.

ABOVE: Bulbophyllum lepidum. A common lowland epiphytic orchid in this part of the world, it flowers freely and is a nice plant to grow landscaped. Different colour forms occur in various parts of the Malaysia. The generic name describes the prominent pseudo-bulbs of the plant.

RIGHT: Liparis lacerata is a common lowland epiphyte on tall trees near streams from Myanmar and Hainan southwards to Indonesia and New Guinea. *Liparis* derived from the Greek *liparos* (fat, greasy, shining) referring to the leaves does not distinguish this genus from other Malesian orchids, but there are 200 species of *Liparis* distributed worldwide and the name may be apt for some of them.

Although they are rather small, *Bulbophyllum lepidum* and *Liparis lacerata* are both very free flowering and they require very little attention if grown attached to trees in the garden.

ORCHIDS AT TWILIGHT

It was almost seven in the evening and making my way out of the National Orchid Garden which was closing, I chanced to look at the trees and saw these two orchids beautifully incorporated into the landscape.

ABOVE: Vanda (luzonica x lamellata) grown into a large clump on a tree.

RIGHT: Dendrobium uniflorum on an exposed branch of a Frangipani.

Fading or Faded Orchid Flowers

The statement that even faded orchid flowers can be beautiful is not made with tongue in cheek. Everything depends on one's point of view. Taxonomists who work with both living specimens and preserved material easily appreciate the beauty of the materials they work on and handle it with great respect. A photographer might do likewise. The great American fashion photographer, Irving Penn used to make a study of fading flowers on the desks of his colleagues and he produced a beautiful book with his photographs of such flowers previously published in the Christmas issues of *Vogue* magazine from 1967 to 1973. Indeed fading orchid flowers are worth more than a casual glance.

ABOVE: Fallen *Cattleya* flower.

RIGHT: Large white *Phalaenopsis*, faded.

Medicinal Orchids

You will not see *Gastrodia elata* (*Tian Ma*) in the wild nor in any nursery in Singapore. But you will find it in apothecaries selling Traditional Chinese Medicine (TCM), and perhaps you may find it in your chicken soup in a fancy, or an herbal, restaurant. Chinese tradition says that since the dawn of its civilization the Chinese people, through the kindness of Sheng Nong, have employed *Chi Jian* (Crimson Arrow), later known as *Tian Ma*, to treat dizziness, epilepsy, dementia, or to assist recovery from stroke. Its usage has continued for at least 2000 years, it being one of three orchids described in the *Materia Medica of Shen Nong* (*Shen Nong Ben Cao Jing*) which was written down during the Han Dynasty (221BC–220CE). Its medicinal role has even earned it a place in popular Chinese herbal cuisine, served with meat as soup. *Gastrodia elata* is a parasitic orchid, entirely dependent on its associated fungus for its food supply, but in turn the orchid transfers some essential minerals to the fungus. Thus while the orchid is a predator, there is actually a symbiotic relationship between orchid and fungus.

BELOW: Gastrodia elata. Chinese Name: *Tian Ma* (Heavenly Hemp); Japanese Name: *Oninoyagara* (Orge's Arrow). Looking at the picture of its underground tubers, the alternative common Chinese name well fits the appearance—*Bai Long Pi* (White Dragon Skin).

RIGHT: Dendrobium hercoglossum is one of the many orchids sold as shihu, another of the three medicinal orchids mentioned in the *Shen Nong Ben Cao Jing*. It is used as a tonic.

TASSEL GRASS

Tassel grass (*Spiranthes sinensis*) is a common geophytic (terrestrial) orchid in cool open spaces from Siberia across Japan, China, the Indian subcontinent and Southeast Asia to Australia, New Zealand and the Pacific Islands. Its familiar looking relatives people Europe, North Africa and North America. It is easily recognized by the spiral arrangement of the small, pink or white, partially opened flowers on its long, terminal inflorescence. The slender, pointed glabrous leaves are arranged in a rosette from a short stem which is supported by numerous fleshy roots. The various species are found in montane grassland and in areas where the land has been disturbed. In Peninsular Malaysia it occurs in Gunong Kali, Cameron Highlands and Genting.

Shoucao (Tassel Grass) is the popular Chinese name. Some scholars believe that this is the first recorded orchid which is mentioned in the *Book of Odes* (circa 6th century BC). The several fancy Chinese names refer to it as a 'Dragon Coiled Round a Post' (*Chinglongchanzhu*, *Jinlongpanshu*, *Panglongshen*, *Longbaozhu*). The Japanese call it *Nejibana* (Spiral Flower). It has a small role in Traditional Chinese Medicine which commends its ability to strengthen the kidneys. The Newari say that it is aphrodisiac.

LEFT: Dendrobium jenkinsii is another variety of *Shihu*.

RIGHT: Spiranthes sinensis (Tassel Grass).

PHARMACEUTICAL INTEREST IN MEDICINAL ORCHIDS

Chinese herbal medicine employs fourteen species of *Calanthe* to treat a variety of conditions which include abscesses, arthritis, toothache, pharyngitis, snake bite, trauma, and pain resulting from stomach ulcers or abdominal distension, but *Calanthe* may not be used by pregnant women. *Calanthe alimaefolia*, *C. davidii*, *C. gracilifolia*, *C. fimbriata*, *lamellose*, *C. puberula* are said to be antipyretic. *Calanthe alismaefolia*, *C. densiflora*, *C. discolor*, *C. manii*, *C. mascula*, *C. puberula* and *C. similes* are used for treating wounds and infected skin. Orchids contain phytoalexins which protect the plants against opportunistic microbes. These compounds are bacteriostatic and fungistatic, not bactericidal, and they are usually ineffective against gram negative bacteria.

Calanthe vestita which is common in the limestone areas of Southeast Asia is employed in Vietnam to treat rheumatism. *Calanthe triplicata* (see page 17) has similar uses in Ayervedic medicine. In his delightful account of the medicinal uses of Indonesian orchids mentioned in his *Amboinscha Kruidbock* (*The Amboinese Herbal*) Georgius Everhardus Rumphius (1627-1702) said that the root of *Calanthe triplicata* was a component of a remedy for swollen hands.

More recently, Japanese scientists in Kyoto reported that two *Calanthe* species contain substances with hair restoring properties. Researchers in North Carolina found that *Calanquinone-A* which they extracted from *Calanthe arisanensis* showed promising anti-tumour activity. The compound has been synthesized. Contemporary research does not seem to be inspired by the traditional medicinal usage of *Calanthe*.

The author does not endorse the use of medicinal orchids but he maintains a scientific interest on their development.

LEFT: Calanthe vestita

RIGHT: Anoectochilus formosanus or *Jinxian Lan* (gold thread orchid) is a beautiful, geophytic jewel orchid with multiple medicinal usages in Taiwan. It contains kinsenoside. The orchid is much sought after and tissue culture has been successfully exploited for large scale commercial production. Numerous laboratory studies have been conducted on crude extracts of *Anoectochilus* and on kinsenoside, but there is no properly conducted, randomized clinical trial involving human subjects.

THE PAST, THE PRESENT AND THE FUTURE

Orchids have made Singapore famous in the past and will continue to do so in the future. Despite the scarcity of land for gardens, there are still many avid orchid hobbyists, and the Orchid Society of South East Asia remains a vibrant organization under capable leadership. The National Parks and Singapore Botanic Gardens maintain superb showcases of orchids and provide assistance to aspiring breeders. Singapore is looking forward to its Gardens in the Bay and to the hosting of the next World Orchid Conference in 2011.

LEFT: This spray of flowers of the Tiger Orchid, *Grammatophyllum speciosum* photographed on June 30, 2009 may be seen as an offering from the past, coming from a clump collected by Micholitz in 1890. The plant is possibly the oldest documented, cultivated orchid in Singapore.

ABOVE: A new planting of the *Vanda* Miss Joaquim. It will only produce a glorious display when the orchid stems exceed the wooden stumps in height, a year from now. When one grows orchids, one is always looking forward into the future with anticipation and confidence.

References

Arditti J (19xx). *Orchid Biology. Review and Perspectives,* I. Ithaca: Cornell University Press.

Averyanov L, Cribb P, Loc PK, Hiep NT (2003): *Slipper Orchids of Vietnam with an Introduction to the Flora of Vietnam.* London: Royal Botanic Gardens Kew.

Beaman TE, Wood JJ, Beaman RS, Beaman JH (2001): *Orchids of Sarawak.* Kota Kinabalu: Natural History Publications (Borneo).

Chin SC (1973), *The Limestone Flora of Malaya, Vol. 2* pp.616-683. M.Sc. Thesis. University of Malaya.

Comber J (2001), *Orchids of Sumatra.* Kota Kinabalu: Natural History Publications (Borneo).

Cootes J (2001), *The Orchids of the Philippines.* Singapore: Times Editions.

Corner EJH (1978): *The Freshwater Swamp-forest of South Johore and Singapore.* Gardens Bulletin Supplement No. 1. Singapore: Botanic Gardens, Parks & Recreation Department.

Cortopassi-Laurino M, Zillikens A (2009): Pollen sources of the orchid bee *Euglossa annectans* Dressler 1982 *(Hymenoptera: Apidae, Euglossini)* analyzed from larval provisions. Genetics & Molecular Research 8(2): 546-556.

Elliott J (ed.): *Malayan Orchid Review Vol. 35-41*, 2001-7.

Elliott J, Tan P, Alsagoff SY, Chew W (2007): *Orchid Hybrids of Singapore 1893-2003.* Singapore: Orchid Society of South East Asia.

Go R, Hamzah KA (2008): *Orchids of the Peat Swamp Forests in Peninsular Malaysia.* Kepong: Peat Swamp Research Project UNDP/GEF Funded (MAL/99/G31), Forest Research Institute Malaysia (FRIM).

Henderson MR (1954): *Malayan Wild Flowers Monocotyledons.* Kuala Lumpur: Malayan Nature Society.

Henderson MR and Addison GH (1956): *Malayan Orchid Hybrids,* Singapore: Government Printing Office.

Kaiser R (1993): The Scent of Orchids. Olfactory and chemical investigations. Amsterdam: Elservier.

Kamemoto H and Sagarik R (1975): *Beautiful Thai Orchid Species*. The Orchid Society of Thailand.

Koopowitz H (2001): *Orchids and their Conservation*. Portland: Timber Press.

Laveriack B, Harris W, Stocker G (2000): *Dendrobium and its Relatives.* Portland, Oregon: Timber.

Motes MR (1997): *Vandas. Their Botany, History and Culture.* Portland, Oregon: Timber.

O'Byrne P (2001): *A to Z of South East Asian Orchid Species*. Singapore: Orchid Society of South East Asia.

Schultes RE and Pease AS (1963): *Generic Names of Orchids. Their Origin and Meaning.* New York: Academic Press.

Seidenfaden G and Woods JJ (1992): *The Orchids of Peninsular Malaysia and Singapore.* Fredensborg: Olsen & Olsen.

Tanaka Y, Htun N, Yee T TA (2003): Wild Orchids in Myanmar, Last Paradise of Wild Orchids. Vol. 1. AA The Foundation of Agricultural Development and Education. drtanakaran@yahoo.co.jp.

Teoh E S (ed.) (1978): *Orchids. Commemorating the Golden Anniversary of the Orchid Society of South East Asia.* Singapore: OSSEA.

Teoh E S (2005): *Orchids of Asia 3rd ed.* Singapore: Marshall Cavendish.

Vaddhanaphuti N (2001): *A Field Guide to the Wild Orchids of Thailand. 3rd ed.* Chiang Mai: Silkworm.

Wood HP (2006): *The Dendrobiums.* Liechtenstein: A.R.G. Gantner Verlag.

Wood JJ (2009): *Dendrobium jiewhoei:* An Enigmatic Member of Section *Calcarifera* from Borneo. Malesian Orchid J. 3 (2009): 117-125.

Yam TW (1995): *Orchids of the Singapore Botanic Gardens.* Singapore: National Parks Board.

Acknowledgements

Many people and organizations played a role in fostering my interest in orchids and the opportunity to take the photographs and research the material for this book: the Director of Singapore Botanic Gardens and the staff of its Library, the Orchid Society of Southeast Asia, Mak Chin On, Koh Keng Hoe, Syed Yusof Alsagoff, Teo Peng Seng, Neo Tuan Hong, Puah Gik Song, Law Moi Hwa, Tan Wee Kiat, Whang Lay Kheng, Joseph Arditti, Rapee Sagarik, Michael Ooi, Robert Ang, Tan Wah Sang, Richard Ng, Tan Lip Seng, Phillip Soh and Wu Dongyun. My son, John challenged me to look at orchids in different ways which enriched my enjoyment of the flowers. Phaik Khuan was always helpful and supportive. John Elliott and Tim Yam very kindly went through the book after it was completed and pointed out details that I had overlooked. I am very grateful to them for their comments. I thank everyone that I have mentioned for their assistance and their support.

LEFT: Trichoglottis uexkulliana is a rare species from Borneo.

ABOVE: Single bloom of *Dendrobium* Najib Rosmah.

OVERLEAF: Vanda Josephine van Brero x *Ascocenda* Somsri Gold.

Paul McCartney &

WINGS

Jeremy Pascall

Hamlyn

LONDON · NEW YORK · SYDNEY · TORONTO
in association with Phoebus

Edited: Pamela Harvey

Designed: Rob Burt

Published 1977 by
The Hamlyn Publishing Group Limited
London · New York · Sydney · Toronto
Astronaut House, Feltham,
Middlesex, England

ISBN 0 600 39394 1

Made and printed in Great Britain by Waterlow (Dunstable) Limited

Contents

YESTERDAY

Popperfoto

The end of the Beatles—from the ashes of which arose the Wings phoenix—was marked, sadly, by protracted legal wrangling and personal bitterness. The disintegration of the world's most successful and popular group was long and complicated but it needs to be told in order to appreciate the very considerable battles that Paul McCartney had to win in order to get Wings off the ground.

It's always difficult to pinpoint change to an exact date but if there must be an anniversary for the demise of the Beatles (and, by implication, for the birth of Wings) then Friday, April 10, 1970 will do as well as any. On that day the showbusiness correspondent of the London *Daily Mirror* reported: "Paul McCartney has quit the Beatles."

He went on to prophesy that "Today 28-year-old McCartney will announce his decision, and the reasons for it, in a no-holds-barred statement." However, he supplied some of the possible causes of the split in advance of the statement. The main one being that Paul was in conflict with the other three Beatles over the appointment of Allen Klein as business manager. "Since the Klein appointment," the journalist confidently asserted, "Paul has refused to go to the Apple offices to work daily. He kept silent and stayed at home . . . He was obviously deeply cut up."

An unnamed friend of John and Paul (who were identified as the main antagonists) was quoted as saying: "The atmosphere is distinctly cool. They do not hate one another. This is just deadlock over policy." The report also mentioned that McCartney intended to bring out a solo album imminently and that he would be declaring: "I have no future plans to record or appear with the Beatles again. Or to write any more music with John."

The news came as a tremendous shock to any Beatles fan. It just could not be believed. In fact, *The Times* of London reported that it wasn't true! "The Apple organization this morning denied reports that Paul McCartney had left the Beatles. Mrs Mavis Smith, of the company's public relations department, said: 'This is just not true.'

"But she agreed that there were no plans at the moment for more recordings: 'This is quite normal. Next month their new LP will be issued. It has already been recorded, so consequently, as there is already material about, there are no new plans.'

"She knew that Mr McCartney intended issuing a statement today on the release of a new recording, but denied that any critical statements meant a real break-up of the group."

The press office at Apple was in confusion at that time, according to a member of it, Richard Di Lello, who chronicled those mad times in *The Longest Cocktail Party* (Charisma Books). Somehow the news of the split had been leaked to the press, pre-empting McCartney's original plan to issue a long statement (the one referred to in the *Daily Mirror* report) with the review copies of the *McCartney* album. To sidestep continual pressures to give interviews, Paul had instructed his press officers to compile a series of questions they thought the newspapers would most want answered, submit them to him and he would write in his responses. This lengthy questionnaire would then be presented to the media with copies of his first solo LP.

Despite press prophecies, McCartney's statement did not, in so many words, say that he was quitting the Beatles. Many of the questions/answers dealt with the making of the album (the full text appears in the Appendix) but some skirted the central issue.

Q: Are all the songs by Paul McCartney alone?

A: Yes sir.

Q: Will they be so credited: McCartney?

A: It's a bit daft for them to be Lennon/McCartney-credited, so "McCartney" it is.

Q: Will Paul and Linda become a John and Yoko?

A: No, they will become Paul and Linda.

Q: Will the other Beatles receive the first copies?

A: Wait and see.

Q: Is it true that neither Allen Klein nor Abkco (Klein's company) have been nor will be in any way involved with the production, manufacturing, distribution or promotion of this new album?

A: Not if I can help it.

Q: Did you miss the other Beatles and George Martin? Was there a moment, e.g., when you thought: "Wish Ringo was here for this break?"

A: No.

Q: Assuming this is a very big hit album, will you do another?

A: Even if it isn't, I will continue to do what I want—when I want to.

Q: Are you planning a new album or single with the Beatles?

A: No.

Q: Is this album a rest away from the Beatles or the start of a solo career?

A: Time will tell. Being a solo album means it's "the start of a solo career" . . . and not being done with the Beatles means it's a rest. So it's both.

Q: Have you any plans for live appearances?

A: No.

Q: Is your break with the Beatles, temporary or permanent, due to personal differences or musical ones?

A: Personal differences, business differences, musical differences, but most of all because I have a better time with my family. Temporary or permanent? I don't know.

Q: Do you foresee a time when Lennon/McCartney becomes an active songwriting partnership again?

A: No.

Q: What is your relationship with Klein?

A: It isn't. I am not in contact with him, and he does not represent me in *any* way.

Q: What is your relationship with Apple?

A: It is the office of a company which I part-own with the other three Beatles. I don't go there because I don't like offices or business, especially when I'm on holiday.

Nowhere throughout the quite lengthy 'interview' are the fateful words "I'm leaving the Beatles" committed to paper. Perhaps, at this point, Paul thought there might still be a reconciliation or that the other three might come round to his opinion of Allen Klein. It's possible that he just couldn't say it straight out, perhaps inhibited by his well-developed instincts for good public relations. Or maybe, after 15 years of such intense work and friendship with others, he found it difficult to finish it by saying brutally: "It's all over."

Whether it was openly declared or not, the release of that statement and the *McCartney* album signalled, effectively, the end of the Beatles. The legal end—the dissolution of the partnership—would not happen for some years, after a great deal of acrimony. The creative end had probably been reached earlier, the seeds being sown during the filming of *Let It Be*, the recording of that album and continued through the recording of *Abbey Road*. (This latter was the Beatles' last recorded work together; although *Let It Be* was released approximately nine months after *Abbey Road*, it was recorded about six months before it. Its release was delayed to coincide with the premiere of the movie in May 1970.)

The reasons for the eventual breakdown are many and varied; too complex to unravel thoroughly. However, McCartney delineated the three broad areas in the 'interview' when he put the split down to "personal differences, business differences, musical differences." Of these the most publicly obvious, the most chewed-over in the media and, probably, the deepest, was the disagreement over business. It was to echo down the years and even keep Paul's Wings clipped long after he had severed every other connection with the Beatles.

National Film Archive

The Beatles—(left to right) Paul McCartney, John Lennon, Ringo Starr and George Harrison.

The Beatles' business problems basically sprang from their incredible and unprecedented success. Also, few of the people who set out in the early '60s to find fame were capable of handling it when it came in unparalleled proportions. This included Brian Epstein who was catapulted from running a modest store chain in Liverpool to heading an international, multi-million organization within a matter of years. As John Lennon said in 1971, when the full extent of the confusion surrounding Beatles' affairs was just being exposed: "Brian Epstein was a beautiful guy. He was an intuitive, theatrical guy. He knew we had something and presented us well but he had lousy business advice. We were all taken advantage of, Brian included."

The trouble was that when Epstein died of a drug overdose in 1967, he left behind an intricate and tangled financial maze into which the Beatles were locked. That year they had signed contracts that tied them tightly together for another ten years. It was this partnership which McCartney eventually had to break. The main burden it imposed was in treating the Beatles entirely as a group; it presupposed they would do everything together, all contribute equally and so all share equally in royalties from records and profits from tours, promotions, merchandizing etc. (It did not include songwriting royalties which were dealt with separately and also became the cause of an epic business struggle.)

When the Beatles split, each to make his own records or pursue his own projects, the contract was still binding. This meant that if George earned—as he did—£1,000,000 in royalties from the sale of *My Sweet Lord,* each of the other three Beatles was entitled to a share of it even though they had contributed nothing to the making or recording of the song. The same went for any fees earned by Ringo as a movie actor and so on.

In December 1973, Ringo expressed this dilemma and explained why they wanted to get out of it in an interview with journalist David Wigg (and included on the Polydor album *The Beatles Tapes*): "It's not fair that I should share in Paul's efforts, or he should share in mine because we don't work together. We all signed those silly pieces of paper when we were lads which kept us together until '76. I could just sit down for the next two years and not work and collect. Any one of us can say . . . 'see you in '76, just send the cheque!' "

While the Beatles were still creatively together this arrangement posed no problem. The death of Brian Epstein welded them into a closer business partnership, forcing them to take control of their own financial destiny because they didn't want to appoint a business manager in his place. Their idealistic and rather naive plans eventually found a focus in Apple Corps Ltd—a record/fashion retailing/movie producing/electronics developing company-cum-arts foundation. It was formed in 1968 to handle the Beatles' own business and recording ventures as well as to recruit and nurture new musical talent and sponsor, support and finance a variety of artistic endeavors that could not find backing anywhere else.

Paul—probably the most energetic in the heady days of Apple's inception—explained their dream to the press. "We want a controlled weirdness. We want to see if we can get artistic freedom in a business setting." Subsequent experience proved they couldn't.

They started with the very best of professional intentions. Each Beatle would go into the office every morning, take care of business—which might be signing Mary Hopkin, organizing helium-filled balloons for peace, handing out money to an entertainer with a plan for children's theater on the beach of a seaside resort, arranging promotion for *The Beatles (White)* album, the first Beatles LP to be issued on Apple—and return home at the end of a 'conventional' working day.

This disciplined existence didn't last very long, however. Soon the Beatles became bored with being businessmen and even philanthropists. In July '69 they summarily shut the Apple Boutique not, as Paul explained, "because it was losing money, but because we thought the retail business wasn't our particular scene." In fact, the whole Apple operation was chaos. It was run along amiably loose lines that made working in and visiting the Savile Row headquarters very pleasant but was not at all conducive to good business practice. While the record side was highly successful—thanks largely to the Beatles' own spectacular contribution but also aided by hits from Mary Hopkin, Billy Preston and Badfinger—the other branches were in total disarray. Nobody ever seemed to know exactly what was intended or who was working on what and to which end.

So ill-organized was its accountancy that by January, 1969—not a year after opening its doors—John Lennon declared to the press: "Apple is losing money. If it carries on like this, we'll be broke in six months." It was quickly becoming evident that the Beatles *had* to find a strong, disciplined businessman—possessing a flair for dealing with the rather bizarre personalities and methods of the record industry—to take over the day-to-day running of their company. They cast around for suitable candidates—even considering Lord Beeching, ex-supremo of British Rail—and after a lengthy search Lennon announced in February '69 that Allen Klein had been appointed.

The next month Paul married Linda Eastman whose father, Lee, and brother, John, were lawyers specializing in show business clients. This introduced the wedge that finally rent the Beatles asunder because McCartney quite naturally sought the advice of, listened to and felt loyalty towards his father- and brother-in-law. Lennon, on the other hand, had met and been deeply impressed by Klein. The choice fell between McCartney's man, Eastman, and Lennon's protegé, Klein. George and Ringo were not sponsoring any candidate.

As Lennon was to remember it—bitterly, two years later, in a lengthy interview with *Rolling Stone*—there was a period when the decision could have gone either way. "I think somebody said let's see Allen and Eastman together, and see how it is . . . John Eastman had already been in. In fact, we almost signed ourselves over to the Eastmans at one time, because when Paul presented me with John Eastman, I thought well . . . when you're not presented with a real alternative, you take whatever is going . . . Finally, when we got near the point when Allen came in, the Eastmans panicked; yet I was still open. I like Allen but I would have taken Eastman if he would have turned out something other than what he was."

Lennon went on to say that he felt that Eastman "despised" him, that the lawyer "blew it" and that he refused even to meet Allen Klein. Paul, on the other hand, was antipathetic towards Klein and his business methods. Klein's reputation was of a blunt, ruthless, trouble-shooter who would brook no obstacle put in the way of getting what he felt was best for his client and himself.

With the two dominant Beatles split into two camps, what followed was probably inevitable. Perhaps the only way the rift could have been resolved was by bringing in a third, neutral, candidate to run Apple. In retrospect—with the hindsight of about four years—Paul acknowledged to *Rolling Stone* that even if he had got his way in the beginning, things might not have worked out too differently. "Had the Eastmans come in like I wanted, the

***Magical Mystery Tour* TV film. Opposite: posing for the press after broadcasting *All You Need Is Love* on the first world-wide satellite TV transmission.**

Popperfoto

others would have feared I was trying to screw everyone for the Eastmans. It would have been a bit hard for the others to swallow, I'm afraid, since the Eastmans were so close to me."

Klein took over the running of Apple on a three-to-one vote and Paul retreated into his own family life. But he could not, legally, withdraw from the Beatles owing to the contractual bonds thrown around them all. Klein was now heading the company in which McCartney had a quarter-share and Klein, acting on behalf of Apple Corps and the others, set out to accomplish three tasks which, he vigorously asserted, would benefit all *four* Beatles.

He determined to renegotiate their recording contract with EMI and succeeded in doing this to everyone's satisfaction. He then tried to buy Nems Enterprises which had been Brian Epstein's company and which still took a 25% cut of the group's earnings. Epstein had left 70% of Nems to his mother, Queenie. She sold this interest to a City of London merchant bank before Klein could act. The bank then bought out Clive Epstein's holdings in Nems (he was Brian's brother). This left the Beatles, through Apple, with a minority holding in the very company that had once managed them.

Popperfoto

Klein's third avowed intent was to take over Northern Songs, the company that owned the copyright of Lennon and McCartney's songs. The two Beatles owned 15% each of the company which had been set up by Brian Epstein and Dick James early in the group's success. It made very good sense for the people who created the product upon which the company was founded to own that company and reap the full rewards of their own genius. Unfortunately, however, Klein was beaten to the post yet again because in April Dick James and the chairman of Northern Songs sold their 35% holding in the company to Lord (then Sir Lew) Grade's ATV. It was swiftly announced that ATV were bidding to control Northern Songs.

There now ensued a straight fight to gain control of the publishing concern by buying up enough shares to own about 50% of the company. On one side was ranged the might of ATV; on the other, all four Beatles were forged together under the leadership of Klein. Month after month through 1969, the battle waged, each side making bigger offers for shares. At one point the Beatles were prepared to pay over £2,000,000 to secure the number they needed and it would have been worth their while because the previous year Northern Songs had made a pre-tax profit of over £1,000,000. By September, the hostilities were over; ATV announced that they had bought enough shares to give them a majority holding. The Beatles had lost.

For McCartney this was a sad blow. The fruits of his writing talent had been sold, even though he owned more shares in the company than any of the other Beatles (over 750,000 valued, since the take-over, at about £1.5 million). He had hated the endless haggling and plotting, the conferences and campaigns. His disgust with it all came out in a song on side two of *Abbey Road* (issued during September '69, shortly after the share battle finished). It was entitled *You Never Give Me Your Money* and complained that:

You never give me your money
You only give me your funny paper
And in the middle of negotiations
I break down

Talking about the song, George Harrison told David Wigg: "Whatever you're involved with rubs off and influences you. Paul wrote it during all the business things that we had to go through to sort out the past. They come out in Paul's song . . . It was written as what we were experiencing—Paul in particular . . . We had meetings and meetings with banks, bankers, lawyers, about contracts and shares. It was really awful because it's not the sort of thing we enjoy."

The internal arguments had continued through this time and when Paul realized the Northern Songs fight was lost (he and the others sold all their shares to ATV in October) he withdrew further from Apple, Klein and the other three. The business fight was, for the moment, finished. But it was not resolved. That would have to wait for a court decision.

Paul McCartney had ascribed the Beatles' break up to two further differences—personal and musical ones. These were, to some extent, interconnected and had to do with the Beatles' rapid and individual development after Brian Epstein's death. They had already stopped touring by 1967 (they made their last concert appearance as a group at Candlestick Park, San Francisco, on August 29, 1966) and so were not constantly in each other's company.

Back in England they started operating as individuals with their own lifestyles and interests, rather than as a closely-knit group clinging together for support against the madness of fan hysteria, imprisoned hotel living and the sheer tedium and exhaustion of being almost constantly on the move. They spent much of late '66 apart, to such an extent that in November Epstein was denying rumors of a split.

By 1967 the Beatles were mainly coming together for special projects—recording, filming—and rapidly developing their own enthusiasms. George was absorbing himself in the music and philosophy of the East, John and Ringo were acting, Paul was being seen as the wealthy young man-about-town, taking in the fashionably cultural events usually accompanied by Jane Asher. All the Beatles were affected by—and, indeed, spearheading—the peace/love/meditation/drug summer but while all four studied the Maharishi Mahesh's Transcendental Meditation, neither Paul nor Ringo were as heavily involved as John and George. (When they all went to India to receive further instruction in the spring of '68, Ringo and Paul left long before the other two, apparently disillusioned by the experience.)

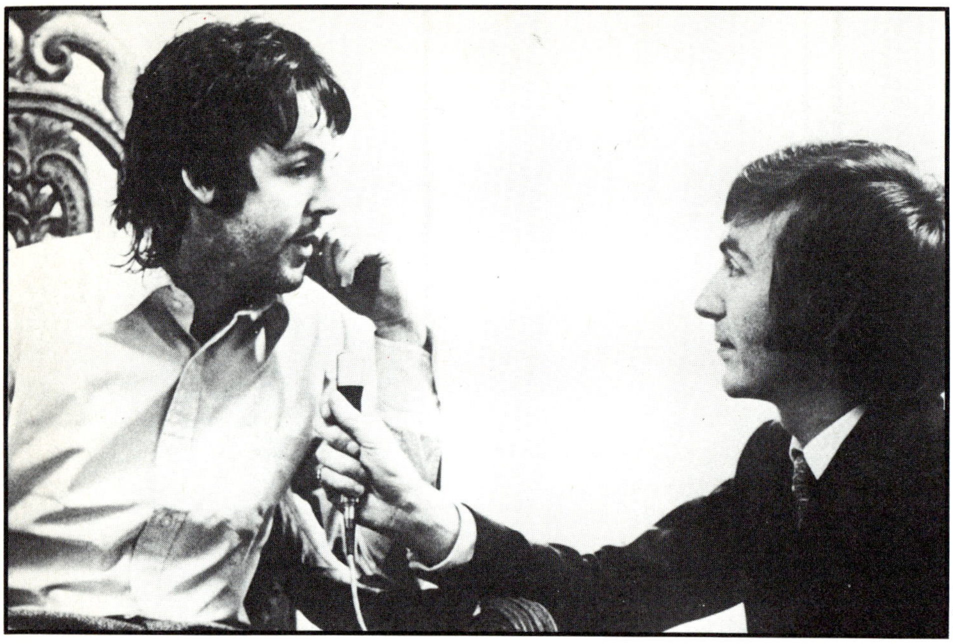

Polydor

***The Beatles Tapes* interview.**

After Epstein's death the group was leaderless and Paul stepped into the breach, trying to give the others a direction and purpose. This led to their involvement in the first critical flop they had experienced since stardom—the *Magical Mystery Tour* TV film. It was his drive and energy that went into making it and, according to Lennon, he assigned the other Beatles roles within the general, loose framework. In his years of antagonism towards Paul, following the court cases, Lennon frequently accused his ex-partner of attempting to dominate the group and this was a charge he laid against him in connection with *Magical Mystery Tour.* He did, rather schizophrenically, admit that it was Paul who had kept the group together following Epstein's death but insisted that both he and George had started to resent McCartney's overbearing attitude towards them.

This was much more marked when it came to music. Lennon once claimed that his songwriting partnership with Paul had effectively finished "around 1962." Certainly they had grown apart increasingly over the years, writing their own songs and occasionally asking for the other's help when a lyric or melody wouldn't work out. Although they shared the credits (and the royalties) it had never been a secret that *Yesterday,* for example, was entirely Paul's creation or *Nowhere Man* was written solely by John. However, it wasn't always that cut and dried and the two certainly worked together on some of the songs on *Sgt Pepper.*

The trend after *Pepper* had been towards albums made up of the four individuals' work and this caused resentments. McCartney has always had the most remarkable and enviable facility for writing melodic, successful songs. It's a God-given talent that allows him to apparently snatch a hit out of the air while others have to graft away at every riff and line of lyric. It also meant that at any time he had a substantial backlog of excellent material waiting to be recorded.

This can be hard on others. As John told *Rolling Stone:* "Paul had a tendency to come along and say he's written these ten songs, let's record now. And I said, 'Well, give us a few days, and I'll knock a few off.' " This prolificacy led to charges by the others—particularly George—that A-sides of singles and album tracks were unfairly hogged by McCartney songs.

There was also a distinct difference in musical tastes in the later years. Neither George nor John expressed any great fondness—indeed they sometimes indicated considerable antipathy—towards such McCartney creations as *Maxwell's Silver Hammer* and others that leant towards the sentimental or whimsical. They felt such songs had no place in the Beatles' repertoire and John is reported as saying "Why don't you give them to Mary Hopkin? The only time we need stuff vaguely that quality is for a single. For an album we could only do stuff we really dig."

John articulated their different attitudes to music styles in an affidavit presented at court hearings in 1971. He said: "From our earliest days in Liverpool, George and I on the one hand and Paul on the other had different musical tastes. Paul preferred 'pop type' music and we preferred what is now called 'underground'."

By winter 1968, *The Beatles (White)* album showed how sharp the musical rift now was. There were songs instantly identifiable as Paul's (for example, *Back In The USSR, Ob-La-Di, Ob-La-Da*—which John reportedly hated—*Martha, My Dear, Blackbird* and others); as John's (like *Glass Onion, Happiness Is A Warm Gun, I'm So Tired, Julia* etc); as George's (*While My Guitar Gently Weeps, Piggies, Savoy Truffle* and *Long, Long, Long*) and as Ringo's (*Don't Pass Me By*). George described the making of that album as "misery" mostly because of musical disagreements which were soon to come to a head over the making of *Let It Be.*

Viewing the *Let It Be* movie with the advantage of hindsight, it seems to pinpoint two areas of tension within the group—the squabbles about music and the intrusion of two 'strangers' into the group—Linda and Yoko. These were dwelt on at length by George, some years after the event.

One particular incident stood out in his mind. It occurred during the *Let It Be* filming and hinged around the way Paul treated him. He testified about it in written evidence given before a London High Court in February, 1971. His account read: "In 1968 I went to the United States [he had been recording an album with Jackie Lomax for Apple] and had a very easy co-operation with many leading musicians. This contrasted with the superior attitude which for years past Paul had shown towards me musically."

He then went on to talk about filming at Twickenham studios. This was not an enjoyable experience because "it was dismal and cold, and we were all getting a bit fed up with our surroundings.

"In front of the cameras, as we were actually being filmed, Paul started to 'get at' me about the way I was playing. I decided I had had enough and told the others I was leaving. This was because I was musically dissatisfied.

"After a few days the others asked me to return, and since I did not wish to leave them in the lurch in the middle of filming and recording, and since Paul agreed that he would not try to interfere or teach me how to play, I went back."

George later expanded on this clash during an interview with *New Musical Express* in 1976: "As soon as we got back together playing (after George's return from the States) Paul went into this 'You do this, you do that, don't do this, don't do that,' and I thought, 'Christ, I thought he'd woken up by now.' He seemed so understanding when he'd sing songs like *Let It Be.* He comes over as sort of hip to that, but when it comes to practicing . . . it was just misery."

The altercation between the two of them was caught by the cameras for all the world to see and George recalled: "That part was so awful for me to see. Where I say, 'Look, I'll play whatever you want—I'll play if you want me to play, I won't play if you don't want me to play—but just shut up with all this.' That was the day I left. For me, that was when I made my decision. It was the final straw."

This fundamental division in the approach to how the group should be making music was further highlighted in *Let It Be.* There's a sequence showing Paul at his most forceful, trying hard to merge the four disparate personalities

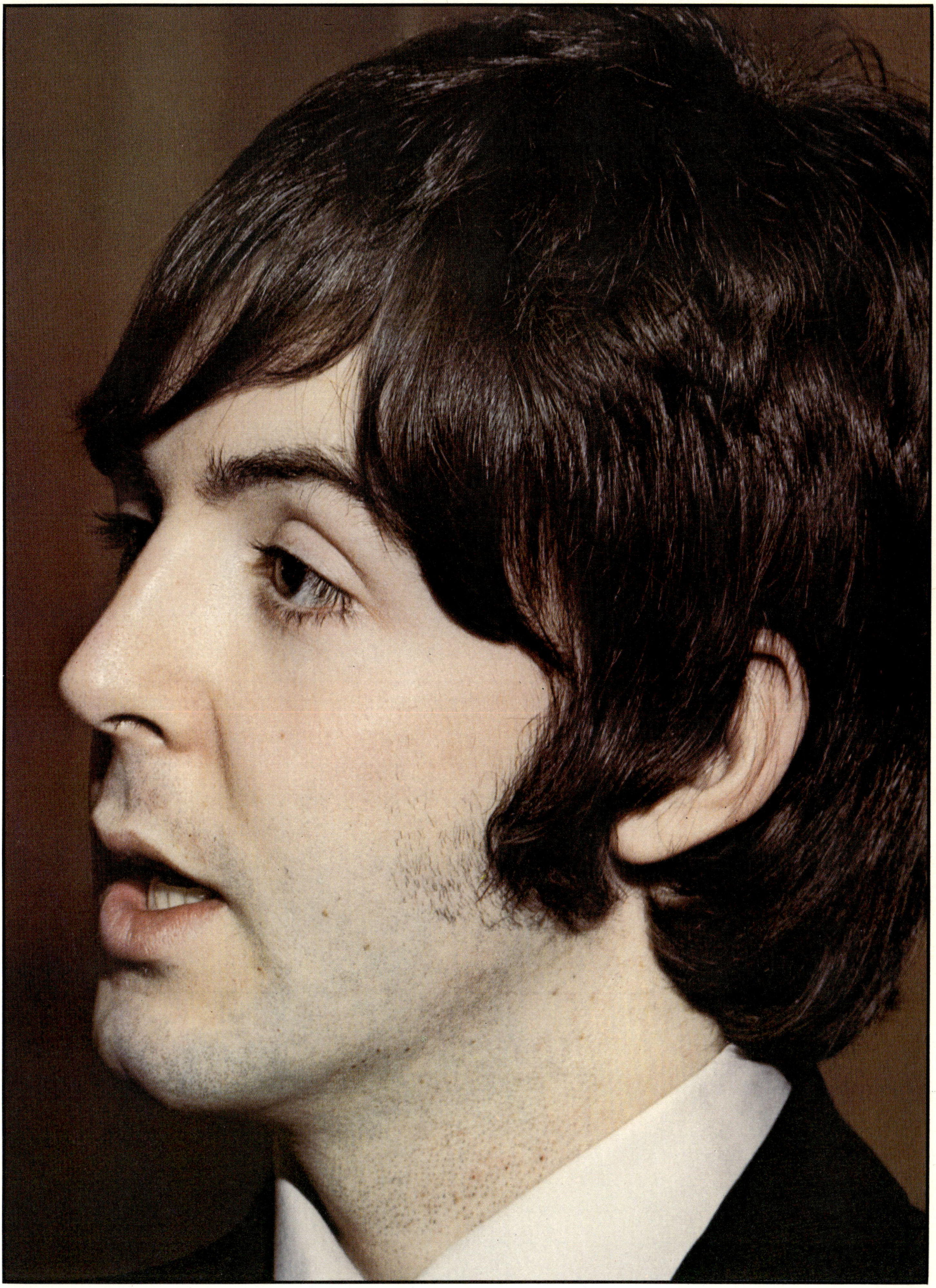

into a cohesive whole. He's attempting to motivate them towards making the movie, to come up with decisions as to the sort of film they want. He accepts the role of spokesman and he does it for the best possible reasons. McCartney really believes in the Beatles and wants to drive them on.

He delivers a lecture to the others and says, in part: "We've been very negative since Mr Epstein passed away . . . we haven't been positive. That's why all of us in turn have been sick of the group . . . There's nothing positive in it. It's a bit of a drag. The only way for it not to be a bit of a drag is for the four of us to think, should we make it positive or should we forget it? . . . It's discipline we need. It's like everything you do, you always need discipline. We've never had discipline. Mr Epstein, he said . . . 'Get suits on' and we did. And so we were always fighting that discipline bit. But now it's silly to fight that discipline if it's your own . . . I think we need a bit more if we are going to get on with it."

This desire of Paul's for organization and order, for getting on with the job and working at it until it came up to his very high standards, became an important factor in his running of Wings. He disciplines himself to work and expects others to match his dedication and insistence on meticulous preparation. He can enforce this sort of regime when the group is demonstrably his own (if the other members don't like it, they can leave). But the Beatles had always operated as a rough democracy, putting decisions to the vote with the majority will prevailing. Previously, they had united against those who tried to govern them. Frequently, they would grudgingly bow to an unpopular Epstein dictate and find relief by resorting to a mocking group humor. Now, one of their own stood up and tried to take the lead and they reacted against him.

These personal antagonisms were exacerbated by the influence of two women—Linda and Yoko. In '68 Lennon was besotted by Yoko Ono and her ideas, fired with enthusiasm to work with her for peace, to create happenings and works of art with her. This love looked, from the outside, like obsession; it was eruptive and sudden. All at once the newspapers were full of reports of their extraordinary doings and they rapidly became objects of public hilarity and abuse. The press seemed unable to grasp what Lennon saw in this "crazy Japanese woman" who shot films of naked bottoms. Their suspicions of the couple's lunacy seemed to be confirmed in November 1968 when they released their *Two Virgins* album which featured a full frontal nude photo of themselves on the cover.

If the press and public's reaction to the Lennon/Ono relationship was incredulous, what was that of the other three Beatles? They, after all, had known Cynthia Lennon for years and must have felt some personal emotion when she

Camera Press

divorced John, citing Yoko. And what were they to make of the astonishing change that had been wrought in him since his meeting with this avant garde artist?

According to John, in his days of bitterness during 1971, the other Beatles "despised her . . . They insulted her and they still do." He told *Rolling Stone*: "You can quote Paul . . . he said it many times, at first he hated Yoko and then he got to like her. But it's too late for me . . . George insulted her right to her face at the beginning, just being 'straightforward' . . . because Dylan and a few people said she'd got a lousy name in New York . . . That's what George said to her! And we both sat through it. I didn't hit him, I don't know why . . . Ringo was all right, so was Maureen, but the other two really gave it to us. I can't forgive them for that."

There's no doubt that Yoko's introduction to the charmed circle was resented, especially when she seemed to assume that she would work with the Beatles. John admitted in the same interview that he was all for expanding the Beatles, broadening them out, trying to turn them on to the sort of avant garde music he and Yoko were making. He also admits that "Yoko was naive, she came in and she would expect to perform with them, like she would with any group, she was jamming, but there would be a sort of coldness about it."

Years later, George looked back on those days and remembered: "Around 1968 everyone's egos started going crazy. Maybe it was just lack of discretion. But a lot of feelings got hurt and probably the biggest problem of all was that there was no way Yoko Ono or Linda McCartney was going to be in the Beatles. That really helped put the nail in the coffin.

"That's said without any bitterness against Yoko or Linda, because I can really enjoy them as people, but let's face it, the Beatles were not with Yoko or Linda. I suppose it was a result of Yoko being an outsider, coming in . . . and John was pushing her . . . and she had such a strong ego anyway. Then Paul got Linda to get his own back."

Much of this internal dissension is exposed in the *Let It Be* movie. By early 1969, when it was filmed, the schisms within the group were apparent and increasing. By the beginning of 1970 the three great factors influencing the final split—business, musical and personal differences—had all reached a crisis. Most of it was still unknown to the public. But on April 10, 1970 came the announcement that Paul McCartney had left the Beatles; on April 17 his first solo album was released in Britain and barely a month later *Let It Be*—which seemed to show the break-up actually happening—was on view. At last, there was proof of the unimaginable, the unthinkable—the Beatles were dead. And, it seemed, Paul McCartney had killed them.

LONG & WINDING ROAD

In 1969 Paul McCartney was dead. He had been dead for three years, killed in a car crash in 1966. The tragic news had been hushed up by Brian Epstein who, according to at least one American underground paper, had recruited a McCartney look-alike. He was called Billy Shears and had been cryptically introduced to the public on the first track of *Sgt Pepper*. Shears—a London musician in small-time bands who had known the Beatles since 1962—needed only minor cosmetic surgery to his "somewhat over-sized, beak-shaped nose" to become Paul's doppelganger.

So great a secret could not remain hidden forever, of course. In 1969 the rumors about Paul's death reached a peak. They were widely broadcast in the States—particularly by a DJ called Russ Gibbs on WKNR Radio in Detroit—were picked up by the other media and were supported by a body of evidence that 'proved' the truth. Proponents of the 'Paul Is Dead' theory claimed that the other three Beatles had leaked hints of the death and Shears's substitution on *Sgt Pepper* and other records and their covers. Apart from telling us about Billy Shears on the *Sgt Pepper's Lonely Hearts Club Band* track, they also described Paul's fatal accident on the last cut—*A Day In The Life*. The man who is described as blowing his mind out in the car is Paul. (Although the most commonly held theory about the identity of the "lucky man who made the grade" is that it referred to Tara Browne, heir to the Guinness brewery fortune.)

A further 'clue' is contained on the back of the *Pepper* cover. A photo shows George, John and Ringo facing the camera but 'Paul' (i.e. Billy Shears) with his back firmly turned against it. Another cover furnished more 'evidence'. The booklet stapled into the British EP sleeve of *Magical Mystery Tour* contains a still on page 23 showing the Beatles in white tails dancing the *Your Mother Should Know* routine. Three of the Beatles wear red flowers in their lapels—significantly, 'Paul's' is black. (More likely the result of bad printing.)

On *The Beatles (White)* album *Revolution 9* supposedly contains the words "I buried Paul" when played backwards. McCartney later refuted this by saying that the words are in fact John saying "cranberry sauce" and that they were on *Strawberry Fields Forever!* The clinching, most conclusive 'proof' of Paul's decease came on the front cover of *Abbey Road*. It shows the four Beatles walking over a zebra crossing in a single file. John leads dressed in a white suit and shoes, Ringo follows in a black suit with a drape jacket, similar in style to a frock-coat. These were said to be "mourning clothes" by the promulgators of the theory. Next comes 'Paul' who is "barefoot and dressed as for burial" (although most corpses are surely not dressed for burial with the double-breasted jacket unbuttoned, tieless and with a cigarette in one hand).

The unshod feet were felt to be particularly significant. Paul had never appeared shoeless before and everyone knows that this signifies a corpse in Eastern religion. Or is it a Mafia sign of death? Either way, it is most revealing. Of course, Billy Shears—in his 'Paul McCartney' persona which he is at pains to preserve—later dismissed the whole thing as bunk and offered the unsatisfactory explanation that it was a very hot day and he didn't feel like wearing shoes. Abbey Road, where the session was shot, is just round the corner from his home in Cavendish Avenue, St John's Wood; it's a short walk and no hardship without shoes on warm London pavements.

The last in this funeral procession was George Harrison who is garbed, so the report has it, in "the work clothes of an English gravedigger." It's difficult to say precisely what uniform is most favored by British sextons; perhaps they *do* incline towards soft shoes, modish blue jeans and denim shirts cut in the cowboy style!

This nonsense continued for several weeks during 1969, despite regular denials from hard-pressed Apple spokesmen. Paul's attitude was to let it run its course until it faded due to everyone's boredom. The rumors were very virulent, however, and grew more insistent. While they were palpably silly and without foundation, they did find their root in the fact that for the past year or so Paul had all but dropped out of sight. He had not allowed any interviews for almost 12 months; this was in itself unusual because he had always been the most publicity-conscious and accessible of the Beatles. He had withdrawn from the press and public alike and, perhaps in petulance, the more fanatical (and ghoulish) of his admirers seem to have started the scare stories to chase him out into the open.

Paul McCartney was actually in retreat from the Beatles and a partnership that was becoming increasingly uncomfortable and restricting. As he later told *Rolling Stone*, "I was playing down a lot of the old Beatles image and getting a bit more to what I felt was me, letting me beard grow and not being so hung up on keeping fresh and clean. I *looked* different, more laid back. . ."

This new relaxation was the other reason for his retirement. He wasn't simply running *away* from the Beatles, he was also running *towards* a new and deeply satisfying phase in his life. He had spent a great deal of time at his farm in Scotland (it was from there, in April,

Popperfoto

Paul and Linda marry on March 12, 1969 in London.

Keystone

A resolute-looking Paul during the Beatles case in 1971.

that he assured journalists of his continued existence) since his marriage to Linda Eastman on March 12, 1969.

On his marriage he immediately gained a family in Heather, Linda's daughter by a former marriage. He found the role of farmer/family man/husband much to his liking and was delighted when on August 28, he became a father for the first time with the birth of a daughter, Mary. He was beginning to relish his new freedom and the close ties of marriage and fatherhood. He naturally wished to be with his family as much as possible. Linda, Heather and Mary provided him with bonds and warmth that he had previously found within the framework of the group.

John was also experiencing this with Yoko whom he married eight days after the McCartneys' wedding. The two 'inseparable' Beatles had now found others to whom they wanted to devote their time and with whom they started to work. Cynthia Lennon looking back on her marriage to John said that in the early days "the Beatles were married to each other, and in many ways the girls were superfluous." That had now changed.

As John and Yoko launched themselves into the campaign of bed-ins and other events for peace, grabbing headlines the world over with their words and, sometimes bizarre, actions, Paul and Linda settled into a period of comfortable domesticity. Paul was no longer working with the Beatles—*The Ballad Of John And Yoko* released in May '69 in the UK and June in the States, was the last recording John and Paul worked on together—but that did not mean he wasn't creating music.

It is impossible to separate McCartney from writing, playing or recording music and now he started directing his activities towards his own projects. He was experimenting with his own equipment in his studio at home and gradually pulled Linda into the sessions. The feel of the new songs was, as he said in that Apple 'interview', "Home, Family, Love."

He was gradually working towards an album of solo work. It was reasonable to expect him to do this as the other Beatles had set the precedent by embarking on individual recordings. As far back as November 1968 George had released the soundtrack album *Wonderwall Music* which he had written and recorded. The same month John and Yoko had put out *Unfinished Music No. 1—Two Virgins* (followed in May '69 by *Unfinished Music No. 2—Life With The Lions*) which heralded a series of independent releases under a variety of headings. First came the Plastic Ono Band with *Give Peace A Chance* in July '69, followed by *Cold Turkey* and the *Live Peace in Toronto* LP. Later there was the *Wedding Album* under the credit of John Lennon and Yoko Ono and later still (in February, 1970 shortly before the release of *McCartney*) *Instant Karma* by John Ono Lennon and the Plastic Ono Band.

Meanwhile, Ringo had been working through November and December 1969 on his own album, *Sentimental Journey,* which was scheduled for release in spring 1970. This, like the others, was intended as a solo venture within the framework of the Beatles and it had never been admitted or even officially hinted at that the Beatles would not eventually come back together to record. Indeed, there was a Beatles album due for release in 1970. It was the *Let It Be* soundtrack and its launch was planned to coincide with the premiere of the movie.

By Christmas/New Year 1970, Paul was almost ready to release *McCartney* but the timing of its launch led to a bitter feud that aggravated the ill-feeling within the Beatles. Ringo's album was originally planned to appear in mid-April with *Let It Be* (premiered in May) to follow shortly after. McCartney wanted his record to come out at about the same time. The other three Beatles were opposed to this. It is a measure of their respect for Paul's music and popularity that they acknowledged his first album would be an important event. Consequently, they were afraid that if it coincided with the issue of *Let It Be* it would harm the latter's sales. They wanted him to hold back *McCartney* until *Let It Be* had achieved its maximum sales potential.

McCartney was adamant that his album should come out close to *Let It Be*'s release date. It's difficult to see why he was so intractable on this point—possibly he wanted to underline his independence by going in against an 'official' Beatles recording—and John later said, rather heatedly, to *Rolling Stone,* "Paul's was just an ego game—it would have killed *Let It Be.*"

Ringo was selected as emissary between the warring factions. John and Paul were already at loggerheads regarding the Klein management and it was felt that Ringo could be an ambassador and take the heat out of the situation. Unfortunately, things had already gone too far and when Ringo went to see Paul a furious row broke out. John later claimed that McCartney "attacked Ringo and started threatening him." In an affidavit read out in court during the 1971 hearings to end the Beatles partnership, Ringo said of that occasion: "I went to see Paul. To my dismay, he went completely out of control, shouting at me, prodding his fingers towards my face, saying: 'I'll finish you now' and 'You'll pay.' He told me to put my coat on and get out. I did so."

Ringo went on to say that he thought Paul had acted "like a spoiled child" but realized that the release date he had set his heart on for *McCartney* had a "gigantic emotional significance" for him. As a gesture of friendship, Ringo persuaded the others to reschedule the launch of *Sentimental Journey,* which was pulled forward by a fortnight and *Let It Be,* which was put back. It was evident that a crisis was imminent.

Shortly after *McCartney* appeared in April '70, Paul told a reporter: "We all have to ask each other's permission before any of us does anything without the other three." This was an intolerable restriction for him. *McCartney* was out and causing a lot of talk, partly because of its 'home-made', fragmented nature, and partly because of Linda's debut as a partner; perhaps a replacement for John?

He had publicly stated—via the Apple 'interview'—that "Linda's on it too, so it's really a double act." And that he expected her to contribute to further recordings because "we love singing together and have plenty of opportunity for practice." Furthermore, he revealed that he had set up his own company—McCartney Productions—which indicated a further break from the Beatles.

He now wanted complete independence to pursue his own musical policies. He felt, he declared, that the album nearly didn't come out "because Klein and some of the others thought it would be too near the date of the next album." He was embittered by the fact that he had to go to one of the other Beatles—in this case George—for him to authorize its release on Apple. The fact that they were all directors of Apple meant that one faction could conspire to block the release of another's work.

Paul could now see only one course open to him. He quit the Beatles. At least, he quit them physically in that he communicated with them only through lawyers. He quit them creatively, but he could not yet quit them legally. That had to be accomplished in the courts and it resulted in one of the saddest, most acrimonious disputes ever to be publicly paraded in the history of rock music.

At the very end of December 1970, McCartney started proceedings in the High Court to terminate the Beatles' partnership. A writ was issued in his name asking that the partnership be dissolved, its affairs wound up and a Receiver—an officer nominated by the courts to operate a company under litigation—be appointed to run their affairs. In a preliminary hearing held on January 19, 1971, McCartney's lawyer told the court that he was seeking the dissolution for three main reasons: 1) The Beatles had ceased performing as a group and therefore the purpose of the partnership had gone; 2) the other three Beatles had appointed Klein and Abkco in breach of the original partnership deed; and 3) Paul had never received audited accounts of the partnership's financial position.

When the main hearing took place a month later, these points were reiterated but the main thrust of McCartney's application was for the appointment of a Receiver. He felt this to be necessary because he believed Allen Klein unsuitable to run the company.

It was a long drawn-out battle, lasting from mid-February to March 12. In the course of it many claims were made, many accusations hurled. Hurtful things were said as the Beatles tore themselves apart while all the world looked on. The majority of Paul's complaints were levelled against Allen Klein. Among other things brought out in court, McCartney's lawyer cited a recent conviction in New York for "unlawfully failing to make and file returns of Federal income taxes."

In defence of Mr Klein, it was stated that he had more than doubled the Beatles' income in the first nine months of his managership and then boosted it by five times the original figure. Claim and counter-claim, allegation and counter-allegation were made throughout the weeks of the hearings. The lawyer appearing on behalf of John, George and Ringo (and who therefore strenuously defended Allen Klein) accused Paul of unreality, of seeing everything in terms of black and white, rather than shades of grey. "Mr McCartney . . . seems to live in a world where everyone is either a seraphim or [devil] . . . where there is precious little room for the intermediate atmosphere in which most people live."

The daily press reports of the proceedings made sorry reading for any Beatles fan. Each new session seemed to bring more anger and frustration, resentment and abuse welling to the surface. How could something that had started so happily and light-heartedly, in friendship and love, end in animosity and disgust, emnity and distrust?

After all the affidavits and statements, the arguments and legal wranglings, the judge made his decision. Allen Klein was temporarily removed as manager; the judge said that there was no evidence at all that he had pocketed any of the Beatles money. But, he asserted, Paul had solid grounds for mistrusting him and Abkco (Klein's company) as they "had received commission grossly in excess of that specified." In Klein's place a Receiver was appointed "not merely to secure the Beatles' assets but to manage the business fairly as between partners, and produce order."

This was not quite the final throw, though. About five weeks after judgment, the parties were back in court again. This time three appeal judges heard that John, George and Ringo were dropping their appeal against the appointment of a Receiver and that they "were willing to let McCartney go if terms over the partnership could be agreed among them." It was hoped that this could be done without resorting to a full trial for the dissolution. Lord Justice Russell commented: "I can only express the court's hope that the parties will come to some amicable and sensible arrangement."

Throughout these convoluted legalities it seemed to the ordinary fan, reading edited reports in the popular press, that Paul McCartney was the villain of the piece. It looked as if he had broken the Beatles up, turned against his old friends and colleagues and caused all these bitter words to flow. During the hearing Ringo had said, in an affidavit read out by his lawyer, that he was "shocked and dismayed" by Paul's actions, especially as he had agreed to a meeting with the others in January 1971 to talk out their differences. But in December 1970 they had received notice of Paul's intention to go to court. "I trust Paul and I know he would not lightly disregard his promise," he added.

Such evidence served all the more to make Paul look like the man who murdered the Beatles and caused greater resentment among many Beatles fans. What they could not know is the anguish such a step caused Paul or how he felt that he really had no alternative but to set these events in motion.

A few years after the event, Paul McCartney tried to put his role in the break up of the Beatles into perspective. It had never been his intention to hurt or destroy the Beatles. His actions weren't a personal vendetta against his three closest friends. He just did not want Allen Klein to be his manager under any circumstances. He was advised that he could sue Klein; this he was perfectly willing to do. Unfortunately to achieve this end he had to sue Apple and that meant, in effect, suing John, George and Ringo. "For two months I sat around thinking, 'I can't do this,' " he said. In the end, however, his desire to free himself from the Klein-connection overcame any other consideration and he took the only course open to him.

In January, 1975 a news item appeared in some newspapers. It wasn't considered to be startling and consequently usually made about one paragraph. This one appeared in the London *Times* on January 10: "The partnership of the Beatles and Co was finally dissolved at a private hearing before a High Court master yesterday, five years after the famous pop group split up. A writ dissolving the partnership has been sought by Paul McCartney since 1971.

"Solicitors said all matters in dispute between Mr McCartney and John Lennon, George Harrison and Ringo Starr had been fully settled."

The last coil in the complex bonds tying the four Beatles together had finally been thrown off. This was the legal rubber stamp that tidied up the mess. But, in fact and practice, the end had come years before. In a London courtroom in 1971 the Beatles had reached the end of their long and winding road. And, at last, Wings were cleared for take-off.

United Artists

ANOTHER DAY

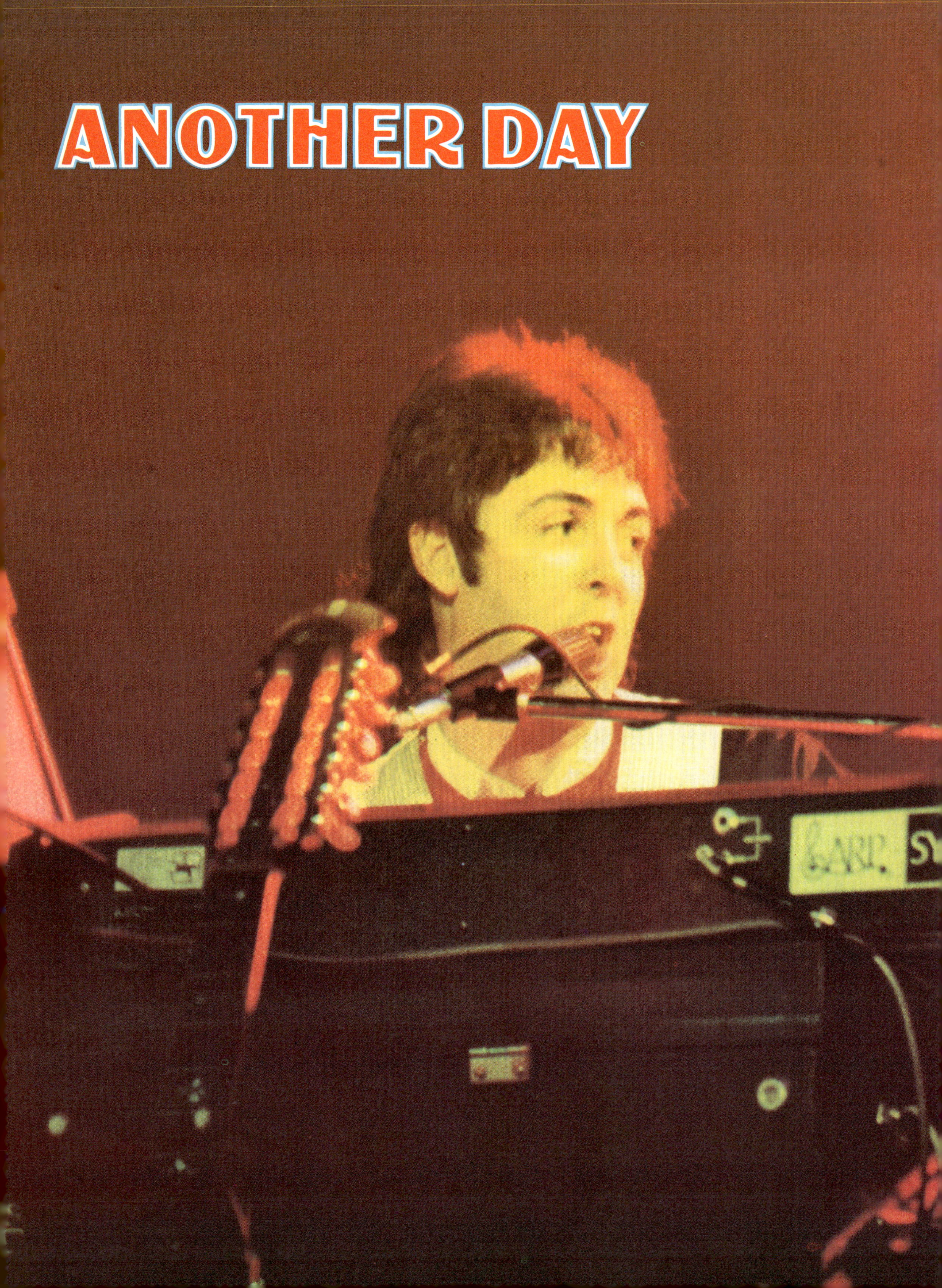

EMI

In the beginning Wings consisted of just two people—Paul and Linda McCartney. James Paul McCartney was born June 18, 1942 (which, for those who place credence on such things, makes him a Gemini) at Walton Hospital, Liverpool, to Mary and Jim McCartney. His arrival was followed in January, 1944 by the birth of his brother, Michael.

His was a close, affectionate family. His mother was a midwife and his father, from whom he most obviously inherited his musical talent, had been a pianist and one-time leader of Jim Mac's Band. They weren't wealthy but, thanks to a working mother, lived comfortably enough in the years of austerity following the war.

Both Paul and Michael were bright boys with quick, alert minds. But Paul soon became bored with lessons and set out on a course of mild delinquency. He was sexually precocious— already very attractive to women by his early teens— and ambitious for the best things in life. Perhaps his drive away from the academic and towards the rebellious was accelerated by the untimely death of his mother. This was in 1956 when she was in her mid-forties; Paul was barely 14.

As compensation for the loss Paul started taking an interest in music, a subject for which he had evinced no enthusiasm previously. He obtained a cheap guitar—strongly influenced by the skiffle boom which showed young people that they could make music on the cheapest of instruments.

His musical ambitions were modest, however, until one summer day in 1956 when he was taken by a friend to a church fete in Woolton, Liverpool, to see a group play. There he met John Lennon—16 and drunk—who was impressed by his knowledge of and ability to play classic rock & roll numbers like *20 Flight Rock*. John saw that this 'kid' could be a valuable asset to his group— who were marked by enthusiasm rather than musical accomplishment—and invited him to join the Quarrymen. Very soon, having exhausted their repertoire of rock & roll standards, the two started writing their own songs.

The Lennon and McCartney partnership was forged and tempered through many years and several groups. The personnel of these bands seemed to change constantly—around the John and Paul nucleus—with particular difficulty experienced in finding a competent, reliable drummer affluent enough to own a kit. On the way, however, they did manage to pick up a promising guitarist in George Harrison. By 1960, the group had more or less stabilized with these three plus Stuart Sutcliffe on bass and Pete Best on drums. The group was known as the Silver Beatles and then, simply, the Beatles.

The full and extraordinary story of the Beatles' rise to rock pre-eminence is too familiar and well-chronicled to need detailed retelling. After gruelling but

EMI

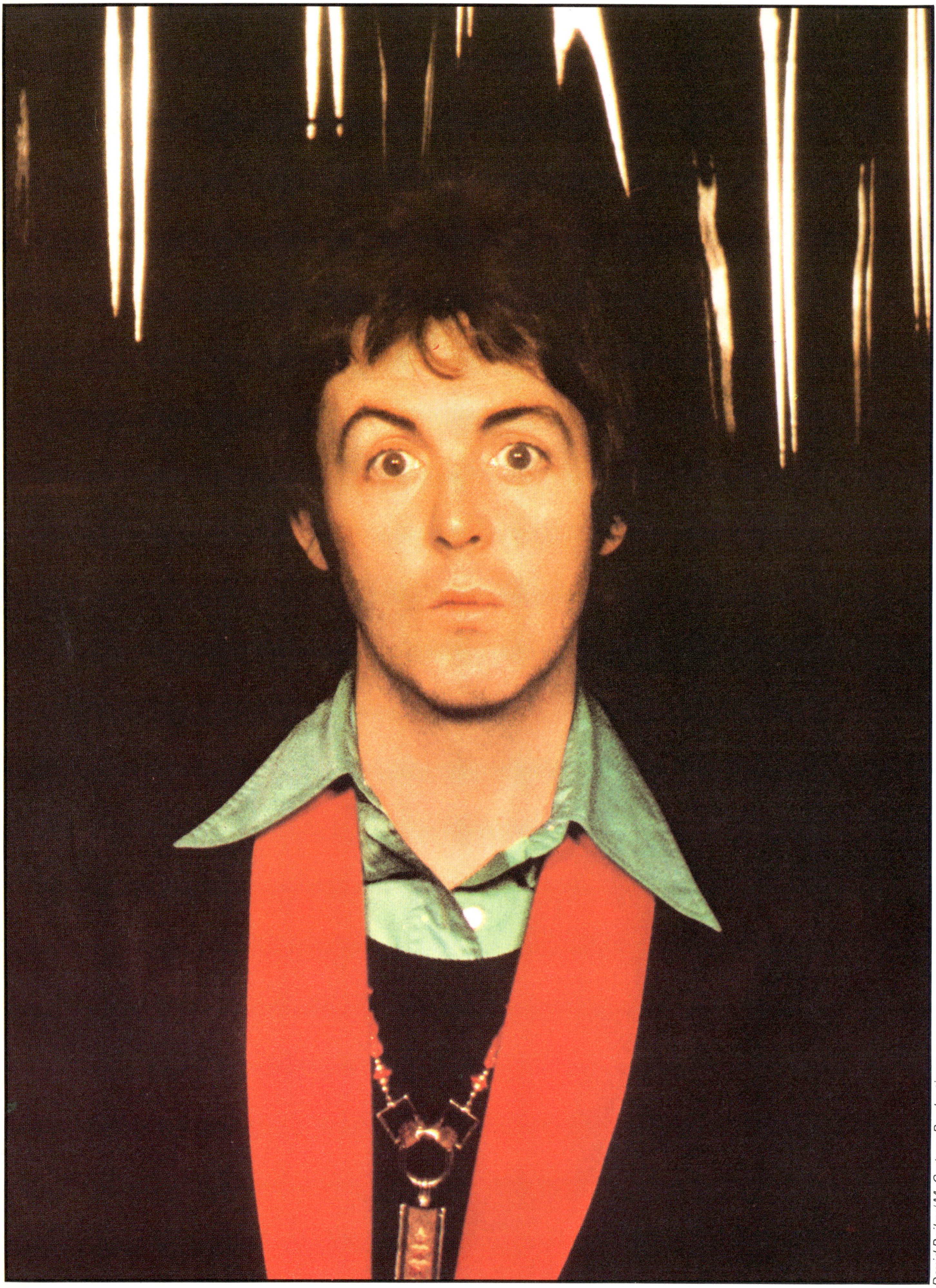

David Bailey/McCartney Productions

valuable experience playing eight hours daily in Hamburg clubs, some minor recording work in Germany backing Tony Sheridan and a growing popularity in their native Merseyside, the Beatles felt they were ready to break nationally in Britain.

Sutcliffe left the band to settle in Hamburg (where he died tragically young of a brain tumor) and McCartney switched to bass playing. They met local store owner Brian Epstein in 1961. He spotted their potential, signed them and used his considerable energy to groom them and push them towards stardom.

After many disappointments, they were signed by producer George Martin to EMI's Parlophone label but Best was regarded as unsuitable, sacked and replaced by Richard Starkey, professionally known as Ringo Starr. The particular chemistry of the Beatles had now found its perfect blend and, after one respectable hit with *Love Me Do* in 1962, the group achieved rapid and alarmingly hysterical British success in 1963. From this point until Epstein's death in 1967, the story is one of continuing and growing achievement. After conquering the States in 1964 the Beatles became the most popular, successful and influential group in the history of rock and, individually, Lennon, McCartney, Harrison and Starr were four of the most famous people in the world.

The impact of the Beatles on the young of the '60s is almost impossible to calculate. They affected every area of youth interest—music, fashion, hair, lifestyle, slang—and impressed their collective personality on a decade in a way that no-one else has ever managed. Perhaps the one quality that made the Beatles outstanding was their tireless pursuit of excellence. Everything they said, sang, wrote or wore, the films and records they made, were different and, invariably, better than anything anyone else had done.

Amid this, they had one great—arguably their greatest—asset: the songwriting genius of Lennon and McCartney. Together or separately John Lennon and Paul McCartney are among the best songwriters in rock. It has been claimed—rashly—that "they are the best songwriters since Schubert." Indisputably, they can, at their peak, be compared with the best composers of popular music like Cole Porter and George Gershwin.

This enviable facility for writing songs that were not only artistically satisfying but also commercially successful made Lennon and McCartney extremely wealthy and, deservedly, gained them admiration and acclaim from critics not normally noted for their approval of popular music. Furthermore, it was allied, in both of them, to fine voices, commanding personalities and inquiring musical minds that led them to experiment in recording and production. Such talents and skills, however, are frequently married to considerable egos.

This was true of John and Paul and was partly responsible for the inevitable clash of opinions and wills and subsequent split. There's no doubt they both regretted the manner in which it had to be done, even if they welcomed the freedom that it eventually afforded them both. Out of the ashes came not just a once-great group, now irrevocably smashed, but four new superstars.

Five superstars if you include Linda McCartney.

Ah, she sings it so
I want to put her on the radio . . .
Ladies and Gentlemen—
a brand new Star

So Paul wrote in *Letting Go* (on *Venus And Mars*) and, consciously or not, it reflects his own actions regarding Linda. He not only married her, but also turned her into a star. The story of Linda McCartney's trip from wealthy American suburbia to hit records and the concert halls of the world is an intriguing one.

It can be said that McCartney was born to music and, by extension, to fame. Linda was not. She was not even born to be—or harbored any ambition to become—a photographer. It was a career—like rock—that she drifted into and succeeded at without having any burning ambition.

Linda Louise Eastman was born three months after her husband on September 24 (making her birth sign Libra), 1942 into a very wealthy family of lawyers. Her father Lee's practice specialized in show business clients and she became blasé about the movie and singing stars who regularly visited their home in Scarsdale.

Scarsdale is a preserve of the well-heeled and successful professional classes in Westchester County, in upstate New York, about 20 miles outside Manhattan. Even by Scarsdale's high standards, the Eastmans were financially very well off, although the story that was constantly repeated in the press that they were part of the Eastman-Kodak photography family has been denied by Linda time and again. She attended Scarsdale High School, said to be one of the best state schools in America, where—for six months or so—Liza Minelli studied.

She shared with Paul a certain youthful rebelliousness. This was later ascribed to a reaction against the high-pressure, go-getting nature of her family's business ethic. Someone who was at school with Linda remembers her as a "quite unhappy kid" who used to like slumming and breaking away from her privileged background. But there's no indication that this took the form of McCartney's petty delinquency.

Although used to entertainers, she showed no early inclination to earn a living from public performance. She shied away from piano lessons—as many children do—and deserted practice sessions for more beguiling activities. On becoming Mrs McCartney and a group member, she regretted this abandonment of musical tuition.

She enjoyed her music at second hand, via radio and records, and quickly became an enthusiastic and knowledgeable pop fan. She later remembered these days saying: "All my teen years were spent with an ear to the radio." Soon she started slipping off, sometimes cutting schoolwork, to see shows at the Brooklyn Paramount. "They'd have 20 acts on 24 hours a day. Alan Freed [the disc jockey described by some rock historians as the Father Of Rock & Roll] was the MC but sometimes they'd get Fabian or Bobby Darin to MC. I remember seeing Chuck Berry sing *School Days* for the first time."

She never thought of taking her interest any further. She entertained no dreams of being a pop singer. "If I'd been a boy I might have thought 'Yeah, I'll be a singer.' But I was a girl and liked Buddy Holly. I was never into Brenda Lee. She had a great voice and so did Connie Francis but I loved the Everly Brothers and Buddy and Chuck Berry."

Despite a tendency to play hookey in favor of rock & roll, Linda graduated from high school as a pretty average middle-class kid of the late '50s. Her high school yearbook shows her looking serious and big-eyed with a neat page-boy haircut. This demureness is contrasted by a description of her as a "strawberry blonde" with a "yen for men"!

Paul and Linda share an unhappy coincidence in that they both lost their mothers; Paul's to cancer and Linda's in an airplane crash. Paul's loss drove him towards music. Linda's towards a premature marriage. Both Linda and her first husband were at university—she studying history and art—and he geology at Princeton. She seldom speaks of it in detail to the press. She once said quite simply: "My mother died in a plane crash and I got married. It was a mistake."

They were undoubtedly too young, as she later acknowledged, and she saw quite quickly that it was never going to work. "When he graduated he wanted to go to Africa. I said 'Look, if I don't get on with you here I'm not going to Africa with you. I won't get on with you there.' So he went. While he was there I really thanked God. I'd met somebody I liked better. So I wrote and said I was getting a divorce. I got a letter back saying 'Let's not.' I said 'Yeh, come on, let's get a divorce.' Luckily he agreed."

It sounds bluntly matter-of-fact but that is almost certainly just her natural reticence about giving too much of herself away to the press. Her philosophy about marriage and divorce was clearly expressed in the same interview. "I really think it comes down to either you're happy or you're not. If you're not you should split and get happy as individuals. If you are happy together, try and keep it."

The marriage finished, she took herself off to Tucson, Arizona where she started taking photographs and found herself mixing with a bohemian bunch of artists. Her approach to photography was always intuitive, relying on her own creative sense of how a picture should be rather than slavishly following technique and the mechanics of using a camera. Her early hit-and-miss efforts whetted her interest in using photography to earn a living. Eventually, she headed back to New York to look for gainful employment for she now had the responsibility of her baby daughter, Heather.

She landed a job as receptionist on *Town And Country Magazine* and was looking for the chance to make her mark. When the break came, she seized it with a bold stroke of opportunism. Invitations flooded into the magazine's office and one caught Linda's eye. It was from the Rolling Stones who invited *Town And Country* to send a reporter along to meet them at a reception held on a boat on the Hudson River. Linda, already knowledgeable and enthusiastic about British groups, was determined that she should go but, lacking seniority or position, had to resort to subterfuge. She phoned the office that had issued the invitation and accepted on her own behalf, without telling anyone else on the magazine.

When the day came she grabbed her camera and light-heartedly went along to the boat. Although she was still no more than an inexperienced and haphazard amateur, she managed to get aboard and shoot the Stones while all photographers were barred. This stroke of luck meant that her shots were in demand from newspapers that had been denied access. Suddenly, Linda was pitchforked from being a receptionist to professional photographer and found that it was a vocation much to her liking.

She showed an aptitude for working with rock people (she became unpaid official photographer for the Fillmore East concert hall) due as much to her ability to establish a rapport with musicians as her eye for the telling image. She quickly landed commissions from *Mademoiselle* magazine and specialized in visiting British stars who were so much in vogue at the time. She soon gained an entrée to their élite circle.

She worked hard at the job, showing a lot of grit in getting to the people she wanted to shoot. Over the years she had built up an inner toughness that was not evident when she first set out. For instance, she was an early fan of the Moody Blues. "I really wanted to photograph them," she later reminisced, "but I never got up the nerve." (A pleasant irony since she was later to play in a group with Denny Laine!) By the mid-'60s that had changed and someone who knew her in those days told the press: "Few girls in New York had that sort of determination and application as Linda had in 1966." And added, "She's a great photographer, too."

Her attitude to photography was very relaxed and informal. She liked to shoot stars to whose music she could personally relate, preferably outside the rigidity of the studio. Her sessions were frequently day-long events during which she and her subject would wander around locations in New York. She didn't like posing the stars, arranging them this way and that in artificial positions. She liked to employ a sort of camera verité technique, snapping off pictures of the subject's natural reactions. This gave her shots a candid, intimate touch, frequently revealing the private personality behind the public face.

Although she was a good and, ultimately, successful photographer, it was never her ambition to hustle her way into the big league. She loved shooting rock stars, mingling with them and attending concerts and would willingly have done it all for free. As it happens, she was getting well paid for having great fun.

Although she met and photographed most of the celebrated British musicians in New York during those hectic years, she did not encounter Paul there. That meeting came in 1967 in London. Linda was in Britain to shoot material on Traffic and went to one of rock's meeting places, the Bag O'Nails Club, in the company of Chas Chandler (ex-Animals, then Jimi Hendrix's manager). Paul was with a group of friends—including members of the Who and the Stones at another table.

They became aware of each other's presence and started, as Paul termed it, "giving each other the eye." What started that evening was continued 12 months later in New York when Lennon and McCartney visited briefly to promote the newly-formed Apple. The visit was followed by another, private one that included a vacation in California. By now a relationship of some depth was forming and, after he had returned home, Paul telephoned Linda to ask her to visit England.

In an interview with the British rock paper *Sounds*, Linda chronicled the rest of the story. "I came over and we lived together for a while, neither of us talked about marriage. We just loved each other and lived together. We liked each other a lot, so being conventional people one day I thought 'OK let's get married—we love each other, let's make it definite.' It was just like that, and that surprised so many people."

It also angered quite a few. A natural backlash from hard-line female fans might be expected. After all, for years they had cherished a secret dream, an impossible hope that one day the most attractive and only bachelor Beatle might be theirs. There was bound to be disappointment and some resentment towards both Paul and Linda. Paul was quite aware that marriage to anybody could be harmful to his career. But, as he told writer Paul Gambaccini (in *Paul McCartney In His Own Words*, Omnibus Press), it was a risk he was prepared to take. "I know a lot of rock & roll stars . . . who will regulate their life to their image.

Capitol

It can mess you up a lot. I know a lot of guys from the old days who wouldn't get married, even if they wanted to. Wouldn't get married because it might affect their careers . . . But the thing is, in a couple of years, his career is over anyway. And he didn't get married, and he went and blew it. So I didn't . . . Although I didn't wish to blow my career, I thought it more important to get on with living."

While both Paul and Linda were probably prepared for the frustrated antipathy of fans, neither could have foreseen the vilification and downright slander that was whispered around the rock world. These calumnies were almost all directed towards Linda.

Both the McCartneys came in for hurtful and often unfair barbs. Occasionally they would be provoked so much that they felt their critics needed answering. After being needled by a journalist from one of Britain's more sensational Sunday newspapers, Linda snapped: "To hear some people talk you would think I flew from America to London . . . just to get hold of Paul. They are so wrong. It was John who interested me at the start. He was my Beatle hero. But when I met him the fascination faded fast and I found it was Paul I liked."

Paul McCartney married Linda Eastman at Marylebone Register Office on March 12, 1969. His brother Michael (who adopted the surname McGear and was one-third of the comedy / poetry / singing group Scaffold) was best man and very late due to a delayed train. Heather was bridesmaid and Beatle aides Peter Brown and Mal Evans were in attendance. (The latter had been assistant, friend and confidant to the Beatles from the earliest days. He died in peculiar circumstances during a police shoot-out on the West Coast in 1976, one of the most tragic casualties of the madness that grew out of the group's unprecedented fame.)

Apple

Lennon parodies the cover photo of Paul's *Ram* album on *Imagine*.

Although the marriage was arranged on the spur of the moment, there may have been two factors contributing to its timing. Linda was pregnant (their first daughter Mary was born on August 28, 1969) and never before had Paul needed someone to help and support him as now. His long, hard, destructive battle for independence was just about to start and Linda would be a constant source of help, sympathy and encouragement over the coming difficult months.

Almost as if to presage the approaching turmoil, only hours after Paul and Linda were wed George and Patti Harrison were raided by police and arrested for possession of cannabis resin. They later pleaded guilty to the charge and were fined.

All too soon after being married, the couple were launched into the first of the several legal hassles that were to beset them all in the next two years. As they went on, it became increasingly clear to Paul that he had to get out and make his own music. But things were so arranged that he couldn't play with the Beatles because of their personal disputes and he couldn't play without them because of their contractual ties. He felt depressed and useless.

"The job folded beneath me," he told the London *Sunday Times*. "Suddenly I didn't have a career any more. I wasn't earning anything and all my money was in Apple and I couldn't get it out because I'd signed it all away."

He took the family and fled up to the peace of his sheep farm in Scotland. He kept so low on the horizon that the 'Paul Is Dead' rumors circulated. It was a very bad time for him; he was isolated from his oldest friends and colleagues and was being alternately hounded and abused by Beatle fans. He turned inevitably to Linda and, increasingly, in on himself. "I stayed up all night, went on the booze, hit the ciggies," he said in the same interview. "I'd lost all my security. I'd no idea what I was going to do. There seemed no point in joining another group. . . . I was out of work."

The depression couldn't dampen his naturally exuberant spirit for long, however. And it certainly couldn't stifle his need to make music. Soon he had to get back to the thing he did best. As he once explained: "My main thing I like doing is singing. I'm a man who sings. A man who sings every day is a man who sings every day. That man is a singer." And that man cannot long be divorced from recording.

Gradually, through the last months of 1969 he started playing around with scraps of songs, tinkering in his home studio and slowly working towards an albumful of material. Now there were no Beatles to help him and so he fell back on his own resources. There was no particular intention to create an album initially. He started experimenting with the newly-installed equipment, using half-completed songs or even just snatches

David Warner Ellis

The McCartney children, (left to right) Stella, Heather and Mary.

to test its capabilities.

The finished result was a fragmented collection that fell into four categories. There were the recently-written complete songs like *Maybe I'm Amazed* that were transitional, linking work intended for the Beatles and songs tailored specifically for McCartney. In addition there were those composed for the group like *Junk* and *Teddy Boy* (both written while with the Maharishi in India and intended for *Abbey Road* and *Let It Be* respectively) and *Hot As Sun* which was from way back in the late '50s. There were several impromptu songs that were improvized on the spot or written in stages as and when needed. These included *Valentine Day, Man We Was Lonely* and *OO You.* The last category comprised oddities like *Glasses* ("Wineglasses played at random and over-dubbed on top of each other. . .") and *The Lovely Linda* which Paul described as "the first song I recorded, to test the machine . . . a trailer to the full song which will be recorded in the future."

Because he was working alone (except for the occasional help of a recording engineer) he naturally called on Linda for musical and moral support. He summarized her contribution thus: "Strictly speaking she harmonizes, but of course it's more than that because she is a shoulder to lean on, a second opinion, and a photographer of renown. (She shot the album sleeve.) More than all this, she believes in me—constantly."

Right from the start of his 'solo' career, Paul was publicly crediting Linda, pulling her towards the limelight with him and making it known that they were a partnership not just in marriage but also in music. This was further confirmed by the fact that the first track on his first album was dedicated to his wife–*The Lovely Linda*.

This meant that the McCartneys were putting themselves up to be knocked down, critically. It also seemed to confirm McCartney's pivotal role in the destruction of the Beatles to the uninformed fan. They became rather unpopular even though *McCartney* reportedly sold a million copies in a month. (However, *Let It Be* broke all previous records for advance orders in the States and *Long And Winding Road*, the single from it, sold more than a million copies in a matter of days. This was a McCartney song which had been given a lush string backing by Phil Spector—much to Paul's disgust.)

Despite the success of *McCartney*, Paul and Linda did nothing in 1970 to follow it up. They didn't even issue *Maybe I'm Amazed*—regarded as the stand-out track by most observers—as a single. (The song had to wait until 1977 for that honor. This was a live version taken from the *Wings Over America* triple set.) It's possible that they were too involved in the legal arguments and too unsure of Paul's exact contractual position to record and release further discs.

Legalities notwithstanding, both Ringo—*Beaucoup Of Blues*—and George—*All Things Must Pass*—issued albums subsequent to *McCartney*. John released *John Lennon/Plastic Ono Band* in December, 1970. It was one of the most agonized and pain-filled records ever made, reflecting John's struggle to come to terms with both the distant and recent past. It is haunted by his loneliness (*Isolation*), the spectres of his acutely unhappy childhood (*Mother* and *My Mummy's Dead*), his difficulty in facing up to his fame (*Working Class Hero*) and his fight to maintain his balance (*Hold On*). The most obviously telling track was *God* in which he lists all the things he no longer believes in, ending with "I don't believe in Beatles" and declares "The dream is over." The songs are cries of despair.

That album heralded the most distressing consequences of the Beatles split—John Lennon's bitter attacks on Paul McCartney in both print and on record. In interviews published during January and February, 1971, in *Rolling Stone* he spoke disparagingly of Paul's role in the break-up and said *McCartney* was "rubbish. I think he'll make a better one when frightened into it." Elsewhere he compared Paul's work to that of Engelbert Humperdinck (the middle-of-the-road ballad singer, not the composer of the opera *Hänsel Und Gretel*!).

Perhaps the most wounding and certainly the most vitriolic and scathing blast was contained in Lennon's 1971 *Imagine* album. It appeared in the US in September (UK release in October), about four months after McCartney's *Ram* LP. The first jibe was relatively good-humored; Paul's sleeve had carried a photograph of him grappling with the horns of a ram, inside *Imagine* was slipped a postcard of John grasping the ears of a large pig.

One track on the album was less jocular in tone. It was entitled *How Do You Sleep?* and it dismissed Paul as a pretty-faced pop star. It maintained that *Sgt Pepper* had come as a surprise to McCartney, asserted that "those freaks was right when they said you were dead," implied that he was surrounded by flatterers and bitingly condemned: "the sound you make is muzak to my ears." It was clearly designed to humiliate Paul and heap scorn on his work, especially his melodic ballads. One couplet (reproduced here exactly as it appeared on the album's inner sleeve) attacked two of his songs, one of which had appeared as a single earlier in the year:

the only thing you done was yesterday
and since you've gone you're just another day

These verbal assaults undoubtedly came out of John's own pain and confusion. They were said or written in the depths of a profound depression following Paul's departure. Even though Paul realized, a couple of years later, that Lennon didn't mean every detail of the insults he aimed at his former partner, the barbs still hurt cruelly at the time. He quite reasonably hated reading each new quote and admitted being deeply wounded by them. Under such a relentless barrage he started entertaining self-doubts, he began to wonder whether the things that John said were true. During this traumatic period Linda had to be ever reassuring, to boost his morale and stop him dwelling too long on his own imagined inadequacies. It was a difficult and unpleasant interlude.

That year had, in contrast, started very well for Paul. His first single, *Another Day,* reached the Top 5 in both Britain and the States and helped further to establish his professional relationship with Linda in the public mind as the writing credit read "Mr & Mrs Paul McCartney." In May the second album, *Ram,* was issued, this time bearing the credit "Paul & Linda McCartney" and Paul confirmed the billing by stating: "Linda was present all the way through. We've been writing many more songs and we're developing as a harmony team . . ."

Ram also marked the start of a bigger team and the gradual formation of what was to be Wings Mark 1. Although Paul had enjoyed working entirely solo (with a little help from Linda) on *McCartney,* he gradually realized that he missed having other people to bounce his ideas off. After all, he had always worked within a group, with a producer and while he could write alone with ease, he found playing and recording in a vacuum more difficult. By the time he was ready to lay down *Ram* he started looking around for help.

He turned first to Linda and introduced her to the keyboard instruments. The first efforts were simple, just getting her to hold the keys down and play basic chords. It was, as Linda later remembered, occasionally rather fraught. "We had a few rows as he tried to teach me. He really put me through it. When everything went wrong I used to say, 'I thought you knew how to make a group?' I never realized how hard it all was."

The easiest course for McCartney was to call in sessionmen, knowing that the very best in Britain and America would willingly drop other projects just for the chance to play with him. But that wasn't his way. Already ideas about a group were percolating through his mind, and he had a conception of the sound. "I wanted . . .*our* sound. I wanted the amateur approach, something we could make ourselves and then work on."

The one area in which he felt he needed assistance was drumming. He's an excellent drummer and has earned praise from Keith Moon of the Who, but it was becoming increasingly difficult to fulfil all the functions. He set up some auditions in New York and, because his standards are so high, he arranged for them to be held under the most trying acoustic conditions. He wanted to find a drummer so good that he could play well whatever the difficulties.

He eventually found his man in Denny Seiwell, a much-in-demand New York sessionman of long and wide-ranging experience. The auditions were held in an unsympathetic, seedy basement that would be any musician's nightmare. Not all those asked to play were very happy about the conditions. "A lot of the boys were really put out at being asked to audition," Seiwell later reported. "Paul just asked me to play, he didn't have a guitar, so I just sat and played. He had a certain look in his eye . . . he was looking for more than a drummer, he was looking for a certain attitude, too. I just played . . . I always say that if you can't get it on by yourself, you can't get it on with anyone."

Denny Seiwell got the job and swiftly found himself playing drums on the *Ram* sessions through January and March, 1971. These led to the release of the album in May. If it was greeted rather coolly by some of the critics, its reception from the public was excellent; it rapidly made number 1 in Britain and 2 in the States. Furthermore, *Uncle Albert/Admiral Halsey* was taken off it and released as a single in America and shot to number 1. (The track wasn't released in Britain where *The Back Seat Of My Car* – a weaker number – was put out and failed to make the Top 20.)

As a result of his work on *Ram* McCartney asked Seiwell if he'd be interested in working as part of a group that he was hoping to form. Seiwell jumped at the offer although both McCartney's music and a group framework were in sharp contrast to his previous experience. Nevertheless, he and his French wife Monique left New York without qualms, moved to a house near the McCartney farm at Campbeltown, Scotland and he became the first recruit to what would eventually be Wings.

Capitol

WINGS TAKE OFF

LFI

Paul wanted to be back in a group. He wanted to feel the internal dynamics of a band at work. He needed to get the feedback of working with other musicians; to build up a song, layer upon layer, as each member contributed something new. But he didn't want to recreate the Beatles. He didn't even want any comparison with them. This time it had to be his own group, one in which he would have the last say.

When he asked Denny Seiwell to join in early '71, he probably only had the vaguest idea about the rest of the band members. Already his choice of musicians was unusual—a complete amateur in Linda and a virtual unknown in Seiwell.

Denny Seiwell might be a name in New York session circles but he meant little to the British rock fraternity. His background, however, was impeccable. He was a born drummer—"I've never practiced the drums," he once said, "I've just played them"—following his father who had earned his living at it until the responsibilities of bringing up a family forced him out.

He started in earnest at the age of seven, playing snare in a boy's orchestra in his home town of Leighton, Pennsylvania and continuing through high school. Rather than waiting to be drafted, Denny signed on for a four year stint in the army as a bandsman. He did a lot of travelling during his service and he was particularly impressed by the Latin American rhythms he learned in Brazil—rhythms that were later to sweep the world as Bossa Nova.

In the early '60s he was out of the army and in Chicago, playing jazz in cellar dives and starting on a long haul towards recognition. He gravitated towards New York and was soon playing the best jazz clubs, gaining the attention of other musicians. His versatility won him a place on the roster of highly-paid sessionmen. This work required him to be able to play in any style and to get it right first time. The pace was hectic: "You get three tunes done in three hours—I've made an album in a day!" But although it was financially rewarding, he found it artistically stifling: "There would be about one session out of every five that was worth playing."

By the time Paul was searching New York for a good session drummer, Denny Seiwell had just about had enough. "I was dying to get out of the studios," he later said. "Everybody was saying I was crazy . . . not taking morning jingles every day. If you don't play live dates the studios can drive you nuts."

After working for McCartney on *Ram* he realized he could fit in with his methods. "It's a nice way to work. When we made *Ram* Paul would run through a song a couple of times, we'd check out a couple of parts and do takes in a few minutes." They worked fast and understood each other. When the possibility of a group was mooted, Seiwell was ready and willing.

And then there were three—bass player, keyboards and drums—although the drummer could also play brass and the bassist could play just about anything you care to name. Now McCartney needed at least one more musician—preferably a good voice for harmony work and an accomplished guitarist. His choice was another Denny—Denny Laine.

Laine and McCartney had been a mutual admiration society for years and often spoke about each other in private conversations and in interviews. Denny Laine was born in Birmingham with the name Brian Hines. He was part of the city's active musical scene and played in a variety of groups with the Brum musicians who would eventually emerge into the international limelight as members of the Spencer Davis Group, Traffic, the Move, Wizzard, Electric Light Orchestra and so on. The Birmingham band that brought him success was the Moody Blues.

Laine (with his raw-edged voice) and the Moodies made one of the classic British hits of the '60s beat boom—*Go Now!* Due to their immaculate image, their tag "The Magnificent Moodies" and their musicianship, they enjoyed a cult reputation in both Britain and America (where Linda Eastman was an early, enthusiastic fan with a burning but unrealized desire to shoot a session with them). Sadly, their chart success did not match their reputation and while they made a good steady living playing Europe on the strength of the one massive hit, they didn't seem to be getting anywhere. Laine, who's always been footloose, left.

He had some unusual and rather advanced ideas about the way that rock in the '60s might develop and he set up as a solo singer/songwriter. Sadly, from leaving the Moody Blues to joining Wings, his several interesting projects never entirely succeeded, either because they were about two years ahead of their time or due to lack of finance.

In the mid-'60s he was signed to Decca's new 'progressive' label Deram (which also recruited the talents of Cat Stevens, the Move and, ironically, the Moody Blues in time for their revival) and caused a great deal of interest in '67 with his brilliant song *Say You Don't Mind.* Both the song and the performance were flawless but somehow failed to catch the public ear. *Say You Don't Mind* didn't achieve the recognition it deserved until five years later when ex-Zombie Colin Blunstone took it to number 15 in the UK charts in 1972. The song was as good as ever but Blunstone's performance lacked Laine's sensitivity. (Decca unsuccessfully re-released the single in January, '72, shortly after Wings' first album was released.)

Denny appeared at one of Brian Epstein's celebrated Sunday night concerts at the Saville Theatre, London that same year with an ambitious project called the Electric String Band. This was a group of classically-trained violinists and cellists whose instruments had been amplified to give a full, rich sound that buttressed Laine's excellent songs. Their debut was complicated by technical problems but showed a great deal of promise and Denny with his superb voice, evident songwriting talents and attractive personality seemed set for stardom. But in this, as in so many other ventures, he was frustrated. "The String Band could have worked," he said years later. "It was way before its time . . .but I just didn't have enough money to play around with."

The next few years saw him involved in several schemes which were interspersed with trips abroad, including a year in Spain, living like a gypsy and learning to play authentic flamenco. He became part of Ginger Baker's ambitious and unwieldy Airforce, collaborated with ex-Move Trevor Burton on the Uglies and poured a lot of time and energy into another group, Balls, that had a shifting personnel including Burton, Steve Gibbons and Alan White before fizzling out after a few gigs and one record.

He returned to solo work again and was working on an album of his own songs when McCartney called and suggested he might be interested in working with him. No second bidding was necessary, he dropped his own material and hastened up to Scotland to meet Denny Seiwell and talk over plans with Paul. Soon they were playing together and laying down the tracks that made up a new album—*Wildlife*—by a new group—Wings.

Wildlife was recorded during August 1971 by a group still without a name. Early in September Linda went into Kings College Hospital for the birth of her third, Paul's second, child. As had happened when Mary was born, Paul moved into the hospital as well, intending to be present at the birth. Unfortunately, there were complications and the baby had to be delivered by Caesarian section. Paul was barred from the operating theater and, as he told the London *Sunday Times,* "I sat next door in my green apron praying like mad . . . The name Wings just came into my head." Linda maintains he was thinking about "Wings of an angel."

Thus Stella McCartney and Wings were born on the same day—September 3, 1971.

Wings released *Wildlife* in December to adverse criticism. Someone had coined the phrase "Suburban rock & roll" to describe *Ram* and the sneers continued. It wasn't a remarkable album and was less popular with the public than its predecessor, reaching numbers 8 and 10 in the UK and US charts respectively. It seems that McCartney recognized that it was not his finest work because no singles were taken from it. He later admitted that "it wasn't that brilliant as a recording." It had been put

Wings Mark 1—(left to right) Denny Seiwell, Linda, Paul, Denny Laine and Henry McCullough.

down in about a fortnight with a group whose members barely knew each other.

One thing that Paul had learned from the *Wildlife* sessions was the need for another musician—a guitarist—particularly as he was thinking of taking the big step of going out on the road and playing gigs. He hadn't played before an audience since the Beatles' last concert in San Francisco in 1966, even though he had tried to persuade the others to tour in the later days. Now he was attracted by the possibility of getting out among the people.

Any guitarist brought into the fledgling Wings would have to be prepared to go on the road. Denny Laine realized this when he joined. "I was ready to go on the road when Paul called me," he later remembered, "and I knew Henry McCullough was too—so I told Paul about him, and that's the way it came about."

Henry McCullough was, and remains, one of rock's more enigmatic figures. His career has been chequered, as he has drifted from band to band, seldom staying long but usually increasing his reputation as a fine guitarist. Born in Ireland, he started his musical life with touring showbands. These are uniquely Irish combos that criss-cross the country, gigging in the rundown dancehalls of small towns and expected to play something to entertain everyone. One number will be rock to satisfy the teens, the next might be a comedy/novelty item for their parents and they may top this off with a traditional air to please the elderly members of the audience.

McCullough stood apart in this milieu, always the long-haired rocker amid the glistening smiles, tacky stage suits and slick routines of his contemporaries. His inclination was always towards rock and eventually he teamed up with some like-minded friends to form the cutely-named Eire Apparent. They, like so many hopefuls before them, trekked across the Irish Sea to find recognition in Britain and, by an extraordinary stroke of good fortune, were spotted by Chas Chandler.

He thrust them into the spotlight by putting them downbill to his major artist—Jimi Hendrix. It was a mixed blessing because it got them—and McCullough in particular—noticed but they were frankly over-shadowed, outplayed and outclassed by the Experience. Things started winding down and, somewhat disillusioned, Henry drifted back to Ireland.

He found further partial success with Sweeney's Men, playing an Irish folk/rock fusion that resulted in local hits but little financial reward. He crossed the sea again and had a further piece of luck in meeting Joe Cocker and joining his Grease Band. Cocker was just emerging internationally and starting to enjoy the rather brief but very considerable success that followed *With A Little Help From My Friends* and *Delta Lady*. Henry accompanied him on the storming tours of the States and started building up a name as a guitar virtuoso.

Just as things were looking good, Cocker—worn down by the strains and enticed by the Mad Dogs And Englishman roadshow—split. The Grease Band struggled on for a while before breaking up. "It was so loose," Henry told the music press after joining Wings. "We could never get anything together; we'd play the same songs every night and they'd always be different."

A man with so much varied experience behind him could only be enticed by an offer to join what was potentially a smash hit group. After all his ups and downs, his near-misses at stardom, Henry McCullough was faced with his best chance yet of making a lasting impression on the public mind.

SKR

The new year that saw Henry McCullough's entry into Wings brought with it controversy. In February, 1972 the group released a single called, unequivocally, *Give Ireland Back To The Irish*. It was McCartney's genuine and heartfelt reaction to the events of Sunday, January 30, 1972—known in Northern Ireland as 'Bloody Sunday'. On that day 13 Catholics were shot dead by British paratroopers after a civil rights demonstration in Londonderry. The troops claimed that they were replying to sniper fire.

There was a feeling of shock and outrage inside Ireland which was shared by many people in mainland Britain, including Paul. He told a reporter that he wrote the song because "the day after the paratroopers went in, everyone thought 'Hey! That's just a bit too much.' "

He admitted that he found himself in a quandary. "If you're in the position of being a songwriter who can make a comment, you're faced with the decision of either saying nothing about it which is fair enough and keeps you cool, or taking the risk of saying something about it and being a little uncool, because it's uncool to say anything political, let's face it."

In the event, he let his emotions rule. *Give Ireland Back To The Irish* was written in the heat of the moment. It was rehearsed and recorded within one day and on sale inside a month. At which point the BBC banned it from the air for its overtly political content. The fact that it wasn't getting airplay did not stop it reaching number 16 in Britain. (It got to 21 in the States. A creditable effort in a market for which it presumably had little relevance.) Nor did it make McCartney regret his stance, even though many were surprised at politics springing from his pen; that was surely something he'd always left to John?

As he told *Sounds* later that year: "Our government happened to be shooting Irish people, and I thought that was real bad news and I felt I had to say something about it. I'm glad I did because looking back on it, I could have just sat through it and not have said anything. But it was just that it got so near home on that particular day I felt I had to say something . . .

"I like the Irish. I dig 'em all. North, South or whatever . . . I've never met an Irishman I don't like . . . The British and the Irish, they're like the same people, particularly for me coming from Liverpool—I'm sure I'm Irish way back somewhere. So it just got to be very personal, the whole thing."

There's no doubt that McCartney's view was not one held by all Britons at that time. And there must have been many—British, Irish or even Ulstermen of both persuasions—who found his views naive. But none could have doubted his sincerity nor the undisguised horror that prompted his song.

Wings didn't have much time to worry about the ban for they were preoccupied with organizing their first public outing together. As with so many other McCartney projects, this was to be unorthodox. He was acutely aware that the group were still getting to know each other and not nearly ready to undertake a full-blown tour that might be expected of a band with an ex-Beatle heading it.

His major problem was that the public would expect so much of him. This was coupled with the fact that he had one completely inexperienced performer in his ranks. Indeed, Linda found it hard to share his enthusiasm for going out and putting on a show. She told the *Sunday Times*: "He went on and on about it, saying he was dying to get back to performing, but wanted me to join in. 'Can you imagine standing on the stage, the curtain going up, the audience all waiting . . .' He made it sound so glamorous that I agreed to have a go."

A further complication was the attitude of the press, expecially the rock media. They'd already been sniping at him for *Ram* and *Wildlife*, there'd been sneers about Linda's role and there would be the unfair but inevitable comparisons with the Beatles' concerts. What he needed was a way of gaining the maximum experience with the minimum amount of press exposure. The best solution seemed to be to take to the road unannounced and turn up to play at previously unbooked venues.

Paul loaded the band, along with assorted wives, children and pets on to a caravan, piled the equipment and a couple of roadies into a van, took to the motorways and headed for whatever university towns took their fancy. Once there they would send in an aide to ask if they could put on a show for the students the next day and, once having obtained permission (who was going to refuse an offer like that?), put the word around the campus. They could set up the gear overnight, go on, do their set, reload the vans and set off for the next town up the road.

The first Wings gig ever—and Paul's first appearance before an audience in nearly six years—was at Nottingham University. The venue was chosen on the simple basis that it was the first they chanced upon. Road manager Trevor Jones once described the organization (if something as casual can be so termed) that went into it: "We went into Nottingham University Students' Union at about five o'clock and fixed it up for lunchtime the next day. Nottingham was the best because they were so enthusiastic. No hassles. No-one quite expected it or believed it. We went down there at half-past eight the next morning with the gear. We threw a few posters up and put the word out on the tannoy."

At lunchtime on February 9, 700 students filed in to watch a new band. "It was 50p at the door," Paul later recounted with obvious pleasure, "and a guy sat at the table taking the money. The kids danced and we all had a good time. The Students' Union took their split and gave us the rest. I'd never seen money for at least ten years. The Beatles never handled money . . . We walked around Nottingham with £30 in coppers in our pockets." Wings were in business.

Delighted with their first excursion into public playing, the band hit the road again and progressed along the motorway until they came to Leeds in Yorkshire. Here the same casual introductions took place again, and here they hit their first snag. As they were starting their set, Paul counted them into the opening number, *Wildlife*, but nothing happened. Linda was paralyzed by fear and quite unable to put her hands on the keyboard. She had advanced stage-fright. Hardly to be wondered at, considering she had been playing keyboards for less than a year, learnt from scratch and was only appearing before an audience for the second time in her life! Paul rushed to her assistance but found that he too had forgotten the opening chords! The students cheered good-naturedly.

As their journey haphazardly continued, a number of university towns reluctantly had to decline their offer due to exams being held or lack of a hall large enough to accommodate the crowds that would inevitably gather. However, by the time the roadshow reached Lancaster University, the press had caught up with the wandering band and was eager to know exactly what the McCartneys thought they were playing at. Relaxed after the tensions of her ordeal in front of an audience, Linda was feeling more confident about meeting reporters and stepped into the front line.

She told *Melody Maker* how satisfied she was with the progress so far. "We've only been playing together for five days and already I have confidence in the band. So far audience response has been good. Surprisingly perhaps I am enjoying these one-night appearances—it's like a touring holiday!"

And what was the reason for the unscheduled gigs? "Well, we just don't like to be tied down. If we wake up one morning and decide that we don't want to go to, say, Hull, we don't have to! With an organized tour your freedom is limited. This is the only way to do it!

"Eric Clapton once said that he would like to play from the back of a caravan, but he never got around to doing it. Well, we have! We've no managers or agents—just we five and the roadies. We're just a gang of musicians touring around."

The adventure proved that Wings were a band capable of performing in public despite its youth and the inexperience of one of its members. Content that they had scrambled through the first phase, McCartney now turned his thoughts towards a more ambitious tour later in the year. In the meantime, the group released the second of three controversial singles that year.

Nobody tried to ban *Mary Had A Little*

Rex Features

SKR

Guitarist Henry McCullough.

Lamb but there were plenty who thought it should never have been released. It could not have been in greater contrast to *Give Ireland Back To The Irish.* The latter was angry and political while *Mary* was a whimsical reworking of an old nursery rhyme. It was as if every accusation hurled against Paul of creating "suburban rock," of being little better than Humperdinck, was coming true.

The fiercely 'anti' reaction to it by the rock press may have taken McCartney by surprise. It's possible that he had not realized quite how incongruous the two last singles sounded. Critics could not understand how the same writer with the same group could come up with two such dissimilar discs. When tackled with this point by *Sounds,* Paul seemed to scratch his head before answering. He didn't have a pat answer to it. His best response was: "I'm crazy. I've always been crazy from the minute I was born . . . Geminis are supposed to be very changeable, and I don't know if that's true or not but I'm a Gemini and I know one minute I might be doing *Ireland* and the next I'll be doing *Mary Had A Little Lamb.* I can see how that would look from the sidelines, but the thing is we're not either of those records, but we are both of them."

If there is one thing that links the two, it is depth of feeling. Both sprang from inside Paul; *Ireland* in anger, *Mary* in love. *"Mary Had A Little Lamb* was just a kid's song," he told the same interviewer." It was written for one of our kids, whose name is Mary, and I just realized if I sang that, she'd understand. That's it with us, that's what you might expect from us—just anything."

In retrospect, Paul was to admit that *Mary* "wasn't a great record." However, he pointed out that it went down well at live shows and that there were quite a few people who did enjoy it. "The quote that sums up that song for me is I read Pete Townshend saying that his daughter had to have a copy . . . I like to keep in with the five year olds!"

During 1972 Paul McCartney declared: "We're just now into a new band. We can see all the new possibilities of working different ways. It's all open . . . it's like a blank canvas." He was keen to start filling in the brush strokes and now looked towards Europe for his next excursion. He was determinedly trying to live down comparisons with the Beatles; he wanted the band to be accepted as Wings and not as ex-Beatle Paul and his little group. He felt that the Continent would perhaps give them a fairer hearing on their own merits and that by playing reasonably large venues there it would serve as a dress rehearsal for full tours in Britain and, ultimately, America.

Although a bigger, more organized tour than the previous run round the campuses, the 1972 tour of Europe still retained a family holiday feel. This time the group travelled in a gaily-painted, open-topped, London double-decker bus, setting off in July to undertake a seven week trip through France, Germany, Switzerland, Denmark, Finland, Sweden, Norway, Holland and Belgium.

This time, they were under the close scrutiny of the British press whose reaction ranged from antipathy to grudging praise. The band's first gig was a modest affair in an open air setting at Chateau Vallon near Toulon in the South of France. Press observers noted that Paul was evidently enjoying himself and that he "commands a respect . . . few others could hope to receive." The 2000 paying customers were described as "enthusiastic but undiscriminating" and while the band generally gained plaudits, one member was singled out for brickbats. "Linda vamps at the keyboard . . . and chirps in with vocals here and there. Unfortunately, her voice lacks both depth and power, a fact which McCartney must know all too well."

The press continued to nip at McCartney's heels throughout the tour, the national newspapers blowing trivial incidents up out of all proportion. One reported: "At virtually every hotel there have been tantrums because the McCartneys will not accept the conventional Scandinavian single beds. The attitude seems to be: 'I want it, therefore it must happen.' " This piece also contained a quote from an unnamed "friend" who said of McCartney: "He lives in a fantasy world. He has been cocooned so long by his money, fame and his own seclusion that he is out of touch with reality."

Other papers—mostly the rock press which is not so bent on sensationalism—noted that Paul was not so out of touch that he couldn't please his audiences. They seemed to enjoy the band and greet it enthusiastically even though McCartney refused to include any song associated with the Beatles in the set. The people who paid money for their seats may have concurred with a critic from one of Britain's national newspapers (even if his tone was offensively blunt) who remarked: "It is no secret that Linda . . . has a voice that can be upsettingly flat and is in the kindergarten when it comes to playing the organ." But they patently did not agree when he went on to say: "Wings, musically, never takes off. At their best they are uninspired. At their worst mediocre. McCartney, wandering minstrel, hasn't made it."

The newspapers had plenty of front page material to splash towards the end of the trip, when the group reached Gothenburg in Sweden. Wings were playing the Scandinavian Hall and at the end of an enthusiastically received set the p.a. system was abruptly cut off by the police who were waiting to question Paul, Linda and Denny Seiwell about seven ounces of marijuana that customs officials had intercepted. It had been sent from London and, they alleged, was addressed to Paul.

Amid scenes of confusion in the dressing-room—caught by the tour photographer Joe Stevens and splashed across newspapers the next day—the three together with Paul's secretary Rebecca Hinds were taken away for questioning at police headquarters. Later a senior officer in the Gothenburg police addressed waiting pressmen: "We told them we had found the cannabis in a letter and at first they said they knew nothing about it. But after we had questioned them for about three hours they confessed and told the truth. McCartney, his wife and Seiwell told us they smoked hash every day. They said they were almost addicted to it. They said they had made arrangements to have drugs posted to them each day they played in different countries so they wouldn't have to take any drugs through the customs themselves."

This version differed in several respects to one offered by the tour organizer, John Morris. He told reporters: "Paul, Linda and Dennis did admit to the Swedish police that they used hash. At first they denied it but the police gave them a rough time and started threatening all sorts of things. The police said they would bar the group from leaving the country unless they confessed.

"The drugs were found in a parcel addressed to Paul by customs men. Lots of people send drugs to the band. They think they are doing them some kind of favor. Instead it causes all this sort of trouble. I'm not prepared to say whether Paul has been posted hash before during this tour or whether he smokes the stuff. It was simply a case of pleading guilty, paying the fine and getting out of the city. As far as we are concerned the whole business is finished."

The public prosecutor of Gothenburg, Mr Lennart Angelin, said that the accused had been released after paying a preliminary fine of about £1000. He explained: "They were not arrested since it was obvious that they were going to use the cannabis themselves and not pass it on . . . They are free to carry on their Scandinavian tour or leave the country."

Paul McCartney was later reported as saying: "The Swedish police behaved correctly. Unfortunately, they take hashish and marijuana far too seriously." An unidentified member of the group was supposed to have said, with surely more bravado than serious intent: "The police action against us was an excellent advertisement. Our name flies now all over the world."

The matter was over and the tour continued but it certainly was not the end of this year of controversy. After the group's return to Britain, a search was instituted by police on the McCartneys'

Rex Features

Scottish farm and, as a result, Paul was ordered in December to appear before a court in March the next year to answer three charges regarding cannabis possession and the cultivation of cannabis plants.

Before the case was heard, Wings issued their third single of 1972—*Hi, Hi, Hi*. And, like the other two, it ran into trouble. It was their second song to be banned in that year. A spokesman for the BBC confirmed that *Hi, Hi, Hi* would be played on neither Radio 1 (the pop station) nor Radio 2 (which specializes in easy listening) because of its content. "The ban has nothing to do with drugs," he said. "We thought the record unfit for broadcasting because of the lyric. Part of it goes: 'I want you to lie on the bed and get you ready for my body gun and do it, do it, do it to you.' Another part goes: 'Like a rabbit I'm going to grab it and do it till the night is done.'"

The irony of this banning lies in the fact that Paul never wrote a line saying "get ready for my body gun." The lyric as he wrote it was "get ready for my polygon." He admitted that it was intended to be suggestive but in an abstract way. He wanted the suggestiveness to be oblique, whereas "body gun" is quite explicit. The confusion occurred because the publishers, Northern Songs, had misunderstood or misheard the lyric and transcribed it wrongly. At first the BBC *were* worried that *Hi, Hi, Hi* might contain drug references and wanted to see the printed lyrics. Instead of drugs they found sex! Or thought they did.

In the event, it hardly mattered because the disc's other side—*C Moon*—was so strong it hit the Top 10 in both America and Britain. Curiously, this number did contain a coded message, but nothing to alarm the guardians of Britain's morals at the BBC. Paul explained it to *Sounds*: "Remember Sam the Sham and *Wooly Bully*? Well, there's a line in that that says 'Let's not be L7'—and at the time everyone was saying 'what's L7 mean?' Well, L7, it was explained at the time, means a square—put L and 7 together and you get a square . . . So I thought of the idea of putting a C and a crescent moon together to get the opposite of a square. So C Moon means cool."

If 1972 had been a traumatic year for Paul McCartney and Wings, the prospects for a peaceful life in early '73 weren't much better. The first major hurdle to be negotiated was Paul's summons to court in Campbeltown to face charges of growing cannabis. The hearing was set for March 8 and the McCartneys flew up to Scotland from London in a hired executive jet to attend.

The court heard that during the previous September a crime prevention officer had gone to the McCartney estate—two farms called High Park and Low Ranachan— to check that it was secure while unoccupied and noticed five plants growing in the greenhouse along with tomatoes. He had become suspicious and, on returning to the police station, had consulted a reference book that had identified them as cannabis. As a result, three charges were brought against McCartney—one of knowingly cultivating cannabis plants to which he pleaded guilty and two others of possessing and having control of cannabis to which he pleaded not guilty and which were subsequently withdrawn.

As in the Gothenburg case,

Joe Stevens

McCartney's lawyer claimed that Paul had received some seeds through the post from a fan. He said that his client had a genuine interest in horticulture. He warned that a conviction on this charge could have serious effects on McCartney's career. "We understand the immigration authorities in the US will refuse admission to a person who has a conviction even though of a relatively technical character," he told the court.

This was no empty warning because in that very month came news from the States that the Immigration Department had ordered John Lennon to be deported from the country as a result of his conviction for possession of cannabis resin in 1968. This presaged John's long, wearisome but ultimately successful fight to be allowed to stay in America. The prophecy came true because Paul could not enter the US for some time and the Japanese authorities refused to let the group appear because of the conviction.

Having pleaded guilty, a conviction was inevitable. When it came to sentencing, the Sheriff—Scotland's equivalent to a County Court Judge—said: "I take into account the fact that these seeds were given to you in a gift but I have to take into account that you are a public figure of considerable interest, particularly to young people, and I must deal with you accordingly. The fine will be £100."

The McCartneys were obviously relieved by the leniency of the sentence and later admitted to pressmen that they thought it could have been worse. Paul jokingly commented: "I was planning on writing a few songs in jail." He then expounded his views on cannabis. "You have to be careful," he said. "I look on it like Prohibition in the old days. It comes up like Prohibition but you have to recognize the law. I think the law should be changed—make it like the law of homosexuality with consenting adults in private. I don't think cannabis is as dangerous as drink." He added: "I'm dead against hard drugs."

March was an eventful month in their lives. On the 18th, Wings gave another of their surprise concerts. This one was at London's fashionable hamburger joint, the Hard Rock Café in Park Lane where they played an hour's set to 200 delighted guests who had gathered for a charity concert. It was held, aptly, to raise funds for Release, an organization which helps drug users and young people in trouble.

A few days later, the group released *My Love*. It was a live recording of the song (dedicated to Linda) that had been laid down on the European tour the previous year. It was more obviously a McCartney product than the three unusual offerings of '72 and quickly became his second (Wings first) number 1 in the States although it only reached number 9 in Britain.

The fact that Wings were more popular in America than Britain (although they hadn't yet played there) was recognized in April when a TV special—*James Paul McCartney*—was screened in the States almost a month before it was seen in the UK. This was a showcase for McCartney and Wings, made at the behest of Lord Grade for his ATV company (which also owned the Beatles publishing company Northern Songs and was associated with McCartney Music Ltd).

The show's contents seemed to reflect the many sides of McCartney's personality and his diverse, sometimes rather confusing, attitude towards the sort of performer he wanted to be. Here a good hard sweaty rocking version of *Long Tall Sally* contrasted with a camp Busby Berkeley-style production number complete with Paul hoofing alongside a bevy of leggy girls; shots of idyllic Scottish scenes competed with the 'working class hero' enjoying a singsong in a Liverpool pub; a solo acoustic rendition of Beatlesque *Yesterday* was offset by Winging *Maybe I'm Amazed*; the rock superstar one minute became showbiz entertainer the next.

The patchwork nature of the film was bound to elicit a variety of opinions. Perhaps predictably, the rock press was largely dismissive of the "cosy, familiar outlook." Britain's *Melody Maker* viewed it rather sourly and opined that McCartney "always had an eye and ear for full-blown romanticism, and nothing wrong with that but here . . . he too often lets it get out of hand and it becomes overblown and silly." One segment was singled out as being "particularly sick-making" in which Linda is photographing Paul while he sings love songs. "The effect is . . . marred a little by Linda joining in with a decidedly flat voice. On the face of it, she does seem to be forever frustrating the best-laid plans of mice and men."

An American critic thought the show "uneven, but it celebrated Paul's various talents. In a visual and musical context the show was an adequate piece of programming and quite an ambitious project." Another rock paper summed it up as "basically light entertainment and no more... a showcase for Paul's amazing ability to be all things to all men, women and little lambs."

Later McCartney was to admit that it was patchy but he strongly denied that he was deserting rock for wider fields. When asked about the Hollywood musical routine (which bore clear resemblances to the *Your Mother Should Know* sequence in the altogether less successful McCartney excursion into TV, *Magical Mystery Tour*) he said: "I suppose you could say it's fulfilling an old ambition. Right at the start I fancied myself in musical comedy. But that was before the Beatles. But don't get me wrong. I'm no Astaire or Gene Kelly and this doesn't mean the start of something big. I don't want to be an all-rounder. I'm sticking to what I am."

The inclusion in *James Paul McCartney* of some songs from his Beatles days—*Yesterday* and *Michelle*, for example—marked a new stage in Paul's development. Until quite recently he had brooked no mention of, or comparison with, the Beatles. Joe Stevens, tour photographer on the European sortie the previous year, remembered being told sternly not to mention the Beatles. "I think he'd been almost brain damaged for a while from having been Paul of the Beatles," he told one publication. And Paul himself told the *Sunday Times* that he "shied away" from Beatles songs at first. "They were too big for us. I knew the audience would be thinking: 'Oh, not as good as the Beatles,'" By now he was feeling a lot more confident about himself and the band.

In between the American and British screening of *James Paul McCartney*, Wings released their *Red Rose Speedway* album which followed the pattern of several of the recent records by going to number 1 in America but sticking at 5 in Britain. It is not one of McCartney's better albums, Joe Stevens declared: "I thought *Red Rose* was a disaster and so did everyone connected with it except Paul."

That's not strictly fair. While Paul is committed 100 per cent to a record when he's making it—as, indeed, he *has* to be—it does not mean that time won't give him a sense of perspective about his work and allow him to see his mistakes. In a newspaper interview in 1977 he said: "Every time I make a record it takes me about three months before I can listen to it . . . After I heard *Wildlife* . . . I thought: 'Hell. We really have blown it here.' And the next one after that, *Red Rose Speedway*, I couldn't stand."

Linda, being slightly outside Paul's intense involvement in every aspect of making their albums, pinpointed the reasons for the record's comparative artistic failure. "*Red Rose Speedway* was such a non-confident record," she said. "There were some beautiful songs... there was *My Love* but something was missing. We needed a heavier sound. Originally the album was going to be a double as we had about 30 finished songs... It was a terribly unsure period."

Speedway's release was part of the run-up to Wing's most crucial test yet—the first full-scale tour of Britain. This was to be the crunch. In the full glare of publicity and with every critic in sight waiting, pen poised, Wings were going to see whether they could make it on the major concert circuit, in front of home crowds who would be as difficult to please as the press. More in some ways because the audiences had the last sanctions—they could sit on their hands, or, worse still, vote with their feet.

It was to be a 17-day, 12-city criss-crossing of the kingdom. Paul realized how vital it was to succeed. In a pre-tour statement he said: "Publicity alone can never do it. The nitty-gritty is the performer clicking. That only happens when the performer has direct contact with his audience."

Wings' flight was to start at the Bristol Hippodrome on May 11 and take in as many major cities as possible. The press were to be formally invited to throw their roses or rotten vegetables (metaphorically) the next night at Oxford. This gave the group the opportunity of a full-scale try-out before being subjected to the public pillories—an understandable precaution when one considers they were playing Britain's bigger venues barely a year after they'd performed their first ever gig together.

Paul was later to assert he was terribly nervous before the tour, but judging by the reactions of the critics after the Oxford show, this was not evident to even the keenest observer. The notices were warm without being adulatory. Best of all, they were generally fair. "If the second night is anything to go by, Paul McCartney's Wings have got off to a tremendous start," said one. "The group gave an extremely tight performance and were able to dramatically raise the pulse-rate of an already enthusiastic audience."

Others commented that the audience were, in fact, rather reserved at first but "that made the band try that much harder." In the end, all agreed, they were won over and responded with genuine abandon and enthusiasm. McCartney had to earn his cheers and screams but that made them all the more worthwhile. This initial hesitancy on the audience's part, a reserve until the band had proved its worth, was a feature of most of the gigs on the tour.

It was difficult to assess how many ticket holders were going in order to see their favorite ex-Beatle and how many were already Wings fans. Linda realized the possibility that many wanted to see Paul but added: "I hope they go away digging it. Paul really digs being in a band. He really loves performing, he loves it to be good and loves things to end up well. He's not into that Beatle trip, none of us are." And while she was aware that there were still jibes against her, she was feeling far more confident than she had on the tour of the Continent the previous year. "I can remember crying my eyes out in a dressing-room in Europe because I was so scared. Now I know you can get up there and have a good time."

Basically, it didn't matter a jot what the press thought of Linda or Wings. The only real critics were those who paid their hard-earned money at the box office. And the true measure of their opinion was the reaction of the most knowledgeable, hardest-headed and least easily impressed audiences in Britain—those in London. And Londoners took to Wings so well during their two storming, bopping shows at the Hammersmith Odeon that a third concert had to be hastily scheduled due to overwhelming demand for tickets.

The tour officially ended in late May but some cities had been missed and weren't at all pleased. So the group arranged four further dates in Sheffield, Stoke, Leicester and Newcastle (and another at Birmingham that had had to be postponed from May). The first real test of Wings as a performing group had been passed with flying colors. They'd at last established themselves in both major areas of rock activity—they could make hit records and they could fill halls.

Meanwhile, Paul was in demand as a songwriter. Roger Moore kept a diary of his experiences while shooting his first film as James Bond. It was later published—*Roger Moore As James Bond* (Pan)—and an entry for early 1973 read: "Paul McCartney has written the song and I had lunch today with the man who is arranging the music, George Martin, who was responsible for so many of the Beatles' hits. It is a tremendous piece of music and I will stick my neck out and say that three weeks from its release it will be number 1 in the charts. It's not last year's music, it's not even this year's music, it's next year's."

In the event, that wasn't a bad prediction from an actor in his forties and, presumably, rather out of touch with rock. *Live And Let Die* reached number 2 in the US charts and 9 in Britain. (The sound-track album by the George Martin Orchestra which featured the song managed, rather surprisingly, to get to number 21 on the US album charts. A good indication of Wings's selling potential.) It was an untypical Wings record in that it was the lushest, most orchestrated and dramatic production they'd done. Its sound was specifically designed to reflect the dramatic, exciting Bond image. Another example of Paul's versatility and willingness to range outside both the rock format and the critics' preconceived notions of the sort of music he should be making.

With the success of this single (it was nominated for a 1973 Oscar) and the other records that year, as well as the triumph of the British tour, everything looked set fair for the future of the group. But just as they were ready to soar, Wings came crashing to the ground. The percipient might have seen storm warnings raised back in April, 1973 when Henry McCullough told *Melody Maker*: "I don't suppose we'll be together for ever, I'm sure Paul's got more of a tie to the Beatles than to Wings." Or when Denny Seiwell offered *Record Mirror* his opinion about a Beatles reunion: "Now that the obstruction in the form of Allen Klein has gone, I should think there's a strong possibility that they will all get together again."

However, both men added that they were committed to Wings. "The band has really progressed as a team," Henry observed. "Everybody wants to make it as a band, whereas before it was just Paul. Wings has all the makings of a great group, but our battle is to keep it as a band and not let it fall apart as it could so easily do. It's worth going at it. I'm there 100 per cent, I know we've got a lot to offer."

Despite these words, by May there was speculation about McCullough's position within the group. The same edition of *Disc* that carried the review of the Oxford concert also ran a news story under the headline: McCullough To Quit Wings? It read: "Henry McCullough... is poised to quit. Whispers at the weekend... suggest that Henry is unhappy and contemplating a return to Joe Cocker, with whom he played as a member of the famous Grease Band." The story went on to quote an unidentified "close friend" who said: "I know Henry was beginning to feel that he could do a lot more musically than he is with Wings. And one person he appreciates more than any is Joe, who is trying to get a new band together."

As the tour progressed, and Wings were seen to be a tight performing outfit, the rumors were somewhat allayed, but shortly before the group was due to record its third album, both Henry and Denny Seiwell quit.

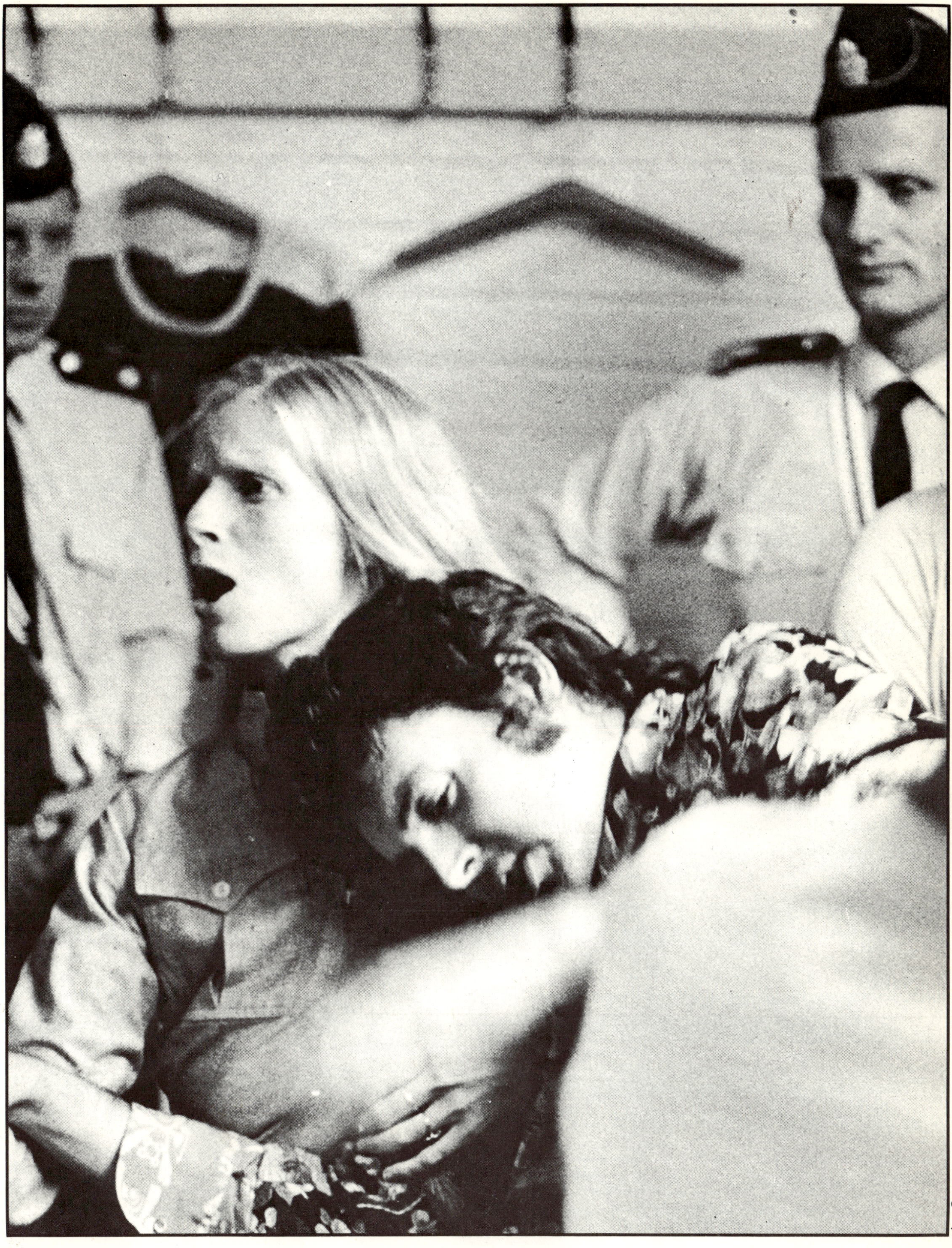

Joe Stevens

While on tour with Wings, in August 1973, Paul McCartney was held by Swedish police in Gothenburg for possession of marijuana, allegedly sent to the group from Britain. Above: Linda protesting on Paul's behalf.

L.F.I.

Joseph Stevens

Main picture: Wings, featuring Paul McCartney in the foreground and Linda McCartney and Denny Laine in the background. Insert, left pic: Linda, Paul and Denny in a London recording studio late in 1973. Right pic: The McCartney family (Mary and baby Stella) cuddled up together on the bus as they wing their way round Europe for their 1973 tour.

Rex Features

The Busby Berkeley-style dance sequence in the TV special *James Paul McCartney*.

Rex Features

Rex Features

The reasons they left are probably many and varied. They are certainly to do with personalities. A group is a complex organism, it depends upon compromises, on people subjugating a part of their personality for the general good. Any group is going to demand that differences are settled quickly and cleanly. In addition there are always clashes of ego (especially among performers) and disagreements about musical styles. Because Paul had been with the Beatles for so long, he had forgotten how fraught the bringing-together of disparate personalities could be. He admitted as much in an interview: "One thing I tend to forget is the people have to more or less live together and if there's a bit of bitchiness on a tour or during something boring like rehearsals . . . We need people who make that side of it very easy for each other . . ."

Henry McCullough had always been something of a loner. His previous record showed that he'd had difficulty slotting himself into a group for any length of time. As Paul said some months after the break: "Henry preferred to lead a more bluesey way of life and he left over musical differences. He was very good at the other stuff but more into blues."

McCullough left shortly before Wings were due to fly to Lagos, Nigeria for recording. He and Paul came to a showdown over styles of playing and he was unhappy about taking directions from Paul. His loss, though sad, was not critical; both Paul and Denny Laine could double on guitar. Denny Seiwell's exit was more dramatic. He phoned to tell the McCartneys he was off only an hour before they were due to fly out. The reason he gave, and Paul passed on to the press, was he didn't want to go to Africa.

It was evidently just the tip of the iceberg and later both Paul and Linda realized that there were deeper motives. A British newspaper quoted McCullough as saying he left because of Linda. "Trying to get things together with a learner in the group didn't work as far as I was concerned," he reportedly groused. Some years later Paul recalled that Henry and Denny would ask why Linda was in the group at all. "I would say: 'I don't quite know. I can't put it into words, but I know there's a good reason for her being here.'"

He said that he was sensitive to their discontents. They felt she was holding the band back. "I could feel this," Linda said. "They thought I was getting the best bits without being any good." It's not difficult to sympathize with McCullough and Seiwell, at least to an extent. It must have been galling for them, as professionals with years of experience, to be slowed down by the faltering attempts of the boss's wife. They were not always alone in that for Paul has revealed: "Perhaps I did have doubts now and again about Linda on keyboard. I did once say to her in a row that I could have had Billy Preston."

After the event the McCartneys could be philosophical about the crack-up of the first band. Linda commented, retrospectively, "That period was almost a relief for Paul. He finally had people with him who cared, those who showed up at the airport. We didn't even know if Denny (Laine) was coming!" And at the time Paul put a brave face on it by telling the press that he wasn't replacing McCullough or Seiwell immediately. The Nigerian sessions were still on. "We are a flexible band and anyway when we are recording I can play the lot myself." For the moment, however, there was no escaping the fact that Wings were broken.

4
BBC tv
colour

BAND ON THE RUN

Redferns

At the Wings' launching party.

Band On The Run—the album that resulted from the Lagos sessions—was a triumph from adversity. It took a great deal of guts and self-confidence for Paul, Linda and Denny to continue with the trip as planned. They were to play in strange studios, in an alien land, without resort to tried and trusted sessionmen.

As if the skeletal group didn't have trouble enough, the circumstances of their stay in Nigeria heaped more difficulties upon them. As Paul later revealed, "It was one of the most frightening periods of my life." Uppermost in his mind was that this album just *had* to do well. Wings were not yet secure enough to withstand fundamental line-up changes and continue gaining popularity. McCartney's name alone could not guarantee sales and success. It was imperative he prove that the nucleus of the band—the creative powerhouse—was able to function unaided.

They were to record at two Lagos studios—one belonging to Ginger Baker, the other to EMI—and hoped, rather piously, to put Nigeria and its rich musical output (which Paul much admired) on the world map. Unfortunately, his efforts were reviewed with deep suspicion by some of the locals who thought he was intending to steal their rhythms, Westernize them and make a commercial success. In the light of the ruthless white exploitation of West Indian reggae their fears could be understood. But it was never McCartney's intention to make an 'African' album. Although he had wanted to, he didn't even try to enlist the help of a Lagos drummer to fill in for Seiwell because of their antagonism and "it would have taken hours to tell him exactly what I wanted, I knew basically that I could do most of it." Indeed, his opinion was that the album had "no particular African influences because I can smell it rather than hear it in the music." By a curious twist of fate, there was one direct African connection. As Paul explained: "The only guy from Africa we used was someone we met in London [drummer Remi Kabaka, sometime of Airforce with Laine], then we discovered he came from Lagos. But that was purely coincidental!"

The antagonism from fellow musicians did not help their already difficult task. No more did the climate. During one studio session, Paul found the atmosphere oppressive, went out for some air but discovered that "if anything, the air was more foul outside than in." Suddenly, he felt an agonizing pain across the right side of his chest and collapsed. He was rather disconcerted to find, upon regaining consciousness, the doctor treating his condition offhandedly. He was ordered to bed where he stayed for some days, "thinking I was nearly dying."

To cap all these troubles, he and Linda were robbed. They had set out—"like a couple of tourists, loaded with tapes and cameras"—on a 20-minute walk to Denny Laine's rented house. On the way a car that had been kerb-crawling stopped in front of them and they found themselves involved in a nightmare. Paul described it to the *Daily Express* in 1977: "The doors flew open and they all came out (there were six) and one had a knife. Their eyes were wild and Linda was screaming: 'He's a musician. Don't kill him.' You know, all the unreasonable stuff you shout in situations like that."

Paul wisely handed over his cash and, mercifully, they were allowed to continue on their way unmolested. On reaching safety they were relieved but unreassured to learn how lucky they were not to have been killed; apparently not an uncommon occurrence in that part of the world.

It says a great deal for Paul, Linda and Denny that in spite of such opposition *Band On The Run* was an artistic, critical and commercial *tour de force*. On its release in December 1973, it met with the first really enthusiastic reviews accorded any McCartney venture since the demise of the Beatles. One critic went so far as to describe it as "the best thing any of the Beatles have done since *Abbey Road*." It became the first Wings record to hit number 1 in both Britain and America. Its worldwide sales were reckoned at 5,000,000, gaining a clutch of gold discs from various countries and it went platinum in the States.

Band thoroughly deserved its success. It's a harvest of delights. Some measure of its worth may be judged from the fact that three singles were taken off it and all became considerable hits. The first was *Helen Wheels* (about the McCartney's trusty Land Rover that bears the same name; it was on the American album but not the British version) which was released as a trail to the LP. Next came *Jet* (named, like *Martha My Dear*, after one of the McCartney dogs); this went into the Top 10 in both the UK and US. Last was *Band On The Run* (backed with *Nineteen Hundred And Eighty Five* in the States and *Zoo Gang*—Paul's theme for a TV series—in Britain) which went to number 1 in America and 3 in the United Kingdom.

The name and cover of the album were both intriguing. The latter showed the three Wings members plus six others dressed as escaping convicts, frozen in the glare of a prison searchlight. The personalities used were all familiar to British audiences but only two—actors James Coburn and Christopher Lee—were instantly recognizable in America. The others were TV chat show host Michael Parkinson, boxing champion John Conteh (like Paul a Liverpudlian), singer Kenny Lynch and gourmet, wit and Member of Parliament, Clement Freud. Later Paul was to deny that the choice of people invited to appear had any significance. They were included, he said, "just for a lark."

In the light of their recent difficulties, was the band on the run Wings? Paul wasn't sure himself. He maintained that it was just a good title, a flowing run of words in a song. But perhaps, subconsciously, he did feel that he, Linda and Denny were escaping from a group in which they'd felt imprisoned. Linda has said that the departure of Seiwell and McCullough was "a relief" and it is noticeable that Wings Mark II has been a happier, tighter and far more satisfying band than the first one.

The enormous success of *Band On The Run* completely overshadowed another Wings-related album released about a fortnight before it. This was *Ahh Laine*, Denny's first solo venture since his involvement with the McCartneys. Many artists would have been frustrated by this but Denny was unconcerned. "To be honest," he told a reporter, "it was rushed off because I was in such a hurry to get back to work with Paul and Linda."

While some others might find working with them difficult, Denny was thoroughly enjoying himself. "This really is the best band I have ever been with. I just know we are going to go right on getting bigger and bigger all over the world . . . I've still got a contract to produce two solo albums a year. But they don't mean nearly as much as Wings to me."

His relationship with Paul was evidently a close and happy one. "We have our arguments but we honestly are good mates . . . The thing is that we both know we need each other—or people like each other—to bounce off . . . With a group you fight about things and it stops you roaring off on the wrong track."

McCartney obviously appreciated and valued Denny's support through the difficult days following the split and agreed with Laine when he maintained in print that "the only basis for anything is a kind of mutual honesty and trust." Denny didn't lose by the lack of time and promotion he was able to give to his own album because as a token of his gratitude for his loyalty Paul gave him a percentage of the royalties from *Band On The Run*. A valuable gift and a generous gesture.

The success of *Band* vindicated Paul's belief in the creative and commercial abilities of his trio. But while they had proved they could make brilliant records, they could not go out on the road in that form. Now, as 1974 was beginning, he had to start the search again for people who could fit both personally and musically into the gypsy family.

He was approaching the selection of his recruits with a once-bitten-twice-shy caution. He wasn't going to rush into anything, remembering the outcome of his last efforts. As he told a reporter, "With the original Wings line-up we took almost the first people we heard who were good . . ." Now they must not only be able to play together but, for quite long stretches in the studios and on the road, live together in harmony.

In December, 1973 he, Linda and Denny had visited Paris to do some recording (notably of Linda's own reggae-inspired song *Seaside Woman* that they intended to release under the soubriquet Suzie and the Red Stripes) and with them, amid much speculation, had travelled Davy Lutton (then playing drums in ex-Love Affair's Steve Ellis' group) and guitarist Jimmy McCulloch. When questioned, Paul wouldn't be drawn into saying whether the pair would be joining the band. His only comment was they'd played together "just to see how it'd feel playing with musicians on a loose, no-strings-attached basis."

The year's turn saw two heartening news items for Beatles fans. The first, in December '73, was the release of *Ringo*, an album on which all members of the former group had worked in one capacity or another. Paul contributed a song and this prompted many fresh enquiries about the possibility of the Beatles reforming. Paul fended these off. About *Ringo* he said: "The others did some stuff for it in Los Angeles and then the material was brought over here for me. I worked on a track called *Six O'Clock* . . . so in a way there's been some collaboration already and I think that kind of thing might happen more often. I'm happy to play with the other three and I'm sure they are too if it was physically possible but more important for me is the new thing because I really get turned on by new ideas."

The reference to the physical impossibility of playing together was the problem that both Paul and John were experiencing as a result of drug convictions. John was fighting to be allowed to stay in America and so dared not leave for fear of being denied readmission and Paul was not yet able to get an entry visa. This led to a rather whimsical plan by which the two would meet at some Canadian border town—each keeping to his own side of the frontier, of course—where they would discuss the still-unresolved Beatles partnership dispute!

Unsurprisingly, nothing came of that but in February, 1974 some newspapers carried an item which stated that a High Court judge in London had approved a scheme to facilitate the continued running of the Beatles' affairs. (This would eventually lead to complete agreement about the dissolution of the partnership.) Paul told reporters that this latest legal step would bring the Beatles closer to working together again. "We've talked about it, but haven't been able to do anything because this has been going on and on." Clearly the acrimony of the past few years was now over.

Paul was also cementing old relationships in other areas. This time family ones as he worked intermittently through January to May producing an album—*McGear*—for his brother Mike. It eventually appeared in the fall of the year and, in addition to production, Paul had written two songs and co-written a further five with his brother and one with poet Roger McGough. Also, McGear's group Scaffold released a single—*Liverpool Lou*—which Paul produced and for which Mr and Mrs McCartney wrote the flip side—*Ten Years After On Strawberry Jam*.

If 1973 was a year of expansion and progress, '74 was to be one of retrenchment. McCartney kept Wings' profile low while he looked for the right people. He was due to record in America during the summer and he obviously wanted to be able to take some compatible musicians with him.

McCartney's visit to Nashville was to be a reasonably relaxed affair. He was to produce an album for Peggy Lee which would include one of his own songs, *Let's Love*. (Both the LP and the title track single were released in October, '74.) He was also looking for a Wings single from the sessions and, of course, tracks for the next album. But he was taking it easy, allowing his guitarist and drummer—both of whom must have felt themselves probationers—to get to know him, his methods and the rest of the band.

It came as no surprise to the music press when guitarist Jimmy McCulloch joined the party. In addition to the Paris sessions for the unrealized Suzie and the Red Stripes release, Jimmy had also worked with McCartney on Mike McGear's solo album. It was at this time that Paul mooted the possibility of McCulloch playing with Wings. Jimmy, with a wake of disbanded groups behind him, needed no second bidding.

Despite his youth (he was born June 4, 1953 and just 21 although he looked about four years younger) Jimmy McCulloch was already a rock veteran. A native of Glasgow, Scotland he had shown a precocious musical talent and set his heart on a career in rock very early. His parents were unusual in that they encouraged him from the start and, knowing that the British rock industry revolves around London, uprooted and moved south to give their son every chance. By the age of 13 Jimmy was playing professionally as the main attraction in a band called One In A Million. At 16 he contributed to a massive hit as part of Pete Townshend's protégé group Thunderclap Newman. The success of *Something In The Air* brought him to the attention of a wider public and he was hailed as an adolescent guitar virtuoso.

As if to prove the point, he was recruited by John Mayall—doyen of British bluesmen and one of the most influential figures in British rock—to step into a line-up that had previously included such luminaries as Eric Clapton, Peter Green and Mick Taylor. To be in such company gave Jimmy a rather premature reputation as guitar hero—a difficult role to play for one of such tender years.

After Mayall, Jimmy was asked to join Stone The Crows as lead behind vocalist Maggie Bell and alongside drummer Colin Allen (later of Focus and Jimmy's songwriting partner for such Wings numbers as *Medicine Jar* on *Venus And Mars* and *Wino Junko* on *Speed Of Sound*). The group was a critical rather than commercial success, a source of frustration to McCulloch who believed it deserved to do well. Nobody can live on praise alone and so, regretfully, Stone The Crows folded and the still-stripling Jimmy looked for yet another musical niche.

The next venture was a contract with Robert Stigwood—one of rock's mandarins—and a group called Blue. This brought him little satisfaction because, in his own words, "the band lacked balls . . . They were very competent . . . but really not my bag. They'd be walking on in Levi's and standing like statues, and I'd be in my white suit leaping around." He drifted out of Blue (but not the Stigwood contract) and rather vaguely into making a solo album of his and Colin Allen's songs.

He was happy to work on a loose basis with the McCartneys and delighted when they asked him to become more involved with Wings because, as he said at the time: "I'm sick and tired of being in and out of bands. I want to get something down on record that's going to be appreciated instead of always being in new bands that so few people hear."

With McCulloch co-opted into Wings, McCartney now set about looking for a drummer. As before, he held auditions but this time in London. One of those applying for a hearing was a tall, lean Cockney called Geoff Britton. He'd played in East of Eden, a band, like Stone The Crows, that enjoyed more reputation than success and followed up as part of the Wild Angels. He'd always, in his own words, "earned enough bread to keep from starvation's door" but had missed the big time. This naturally depressed him, particularly when East of Eden didn't hit. "A great band who never made it and should have," he said ruefully. "It must have been mismanagement . . . because so many of the bands like Yes and Free who were on that circuit at the same time as us *did* make it."

The audition for Wings was something of an ordeal. Britton's name was on a list with about 50 others. He went along to the audition hall and was taken aback by the competition: "You should have seen the people there. It was like a Who's Who of the music industry." Fighting the urge to give it up as a no-hoper there and then, he decided to have a go. "I was a bit disappointed actually because I thought it would be a chance to play with McCartney, but they'd hired session men instead," he told *Disc*, subsequently. "Wings just sat out in front in the audience bit of this theater and watched.

"I wasn't really nervous. I'm never nervous, although I might be a bit apprehensive. We had to play about four

Together again: Paul and Linda are pictured chatting to another ex-Beatle—Ringo Starr—at a reception.

numbers—some of it quite advanced stuff for an ordinary rock & roll drummer. Anyway, I got up there and did my stuff . . . A few days later I got this phone call and they said I was on the short-list of five, and this time it would be Paul and the group playing. That time I had a 20 per cent chance, yet I felt it was more hopeless than ever.

"I met Paul and the group and they were really nice. Anyway, after that I got a phone call saying they'd narrowed it down to two geezers. Each of us spent a whole day with the group and had dinner with them. Then one day . . . the phone rang. It was Paul. He said 'Well, we've decided,' and he was mucking about, geeing me up . . . In the end I said: 'Well, who's it gonna be?' and he said: 'You got the job.' "

McCulloch and Britton were in but there had been no official announcement of the fact, no confirmation to the press that they were fully-fledged Wings members. The five went off to Nashville to record and learn about each other for seven weeks during June, July and August. The result of the visit—apart from the Peggy Lee album—was a Wings single, *Junior's Farm/Sally G*, and a curiosity called *Walking In The Park With Eloise* by a band called the Country Hams.

Linda told *Sounds* the intriguing story behind this when they'd returned from the trip. It was an instrumental of a tune written years before by James McCartney. "When Paul was a little boy, about 10 . . . he remembers sitting at the foot of the piano while his dad was playing this song. We were having dinner with Chet Atkins, the guitar player, one night in Nashville, and Paul had been playing a lot of his music for Chet and he said: 'Here's one that my dad wrote a long time ago'—and he started playing it.

"Chet got talking to Paul, saying that the song should be recorded and that it would be nice for his dad . . . So we got Chet playing on it and Floyd Cramer the piano player and Chet got together a nice little band called Country Hams with lots of other Nashville people."

It was a charming and affectionate gesture and, as Paul told *Disc*, his father was touched by it. "He loved having a record out—but he's very shy . . . and he didn't like all the publicity. I remember him being very emotional about it when I first played it to him—he said I really shouldn't have bothered, but I know he enjoyed it. And do you know what? My Uncle Joe has now written some words to go with it . . ."

Although the Nashville excursion was designed to be an unpressured, get-to-know-each-other period (only about five tracks resulted from it), on the group's return to Britain there were virulent rumors in circulation about the band's internal relationships. *New Musical Express* carried a news story in August, 1974 under the headline WINGS UPHEAVAL. The opening paragraph read: "The existing line-up of Paul McCartney's Wings appeared this week to have broken up, following what is understood to have been a major internal policy disagreement. Sources close to the band suggest that Denny Laine and the two 'unofficial' members, guitarist Jimmy McCulloch and drummer Jeff Britten (*sic*), are no longer working with Wings. A spokesman for Laine confirmed that there had been 'personal difficulties', while another contact stated emphatically: 'Wings have split—the old band doesn't exist any more.' "

Coming hardly a year after the departure of Seiwell and McCullough and months after the drafting of McCulloch and Britton, this was a bombshell. The surprise was further compounded by the allegations that Denny Laine—Wings' most loyal and consistent member—had fallen out with the McCartneys. The details behind the story were confused and not helped by "a Wings spokes-

EMI

Right: Geoff Britton and Jimmy McCulloch.

man" who issued a non-committal statement. It said: "Wings members are free to pursue their own musical careers. This will enable them to develop working relationships free of contractual ties. In future Wings will have a fluid concept, which will be adapted to suit current and future projects."

A *New Musical Express* reporter pressed the spokesman to confirm or deny that Wings had split and elicited this response: "It is wrong to say that Wings are no more, because Wings are Paul and Linda McCartney." In answer to a further question about whether the three would be working with Wings in the future, came: "It depends on their availability. Maybe they will if they are free when Paul wants them—if not, he would presumably engage someone else. As I have already stated, Wings in future will have a fluid concept."

The tone of the story—and the spokesman's hazy reaction—implied that there had been some furious arguments in Nashville. Following-up the *New Musical Express*'s dramatic 'revelation', a journalist from *Sounds* put it to Denny Laine that there had been "a showdown" in America. "No, that's a bit dramatic because it's not that these things hadn't been said before," was the reply. "Various things were said, like they're said in any group—you can't deny that. You know how it is . . . you say something and if someone else doesn't respond to what you're saying then you're walking out, but the next minute you can be walking back. People have been thinking that finally I've said my piece, but that's not true—I just said my piece about what was happening at this time."

Denny didn't go into the specifics of any disagreements there may have been between the McCartneys and the other three although he acknowledged that he and Paul had different ways of approaching their work but, he said realistically, "it was Paul's group, and there was no getting away from that." A further complication sprang from Paul being who he is—one of the most famous men in rock. "There'll always be a difference between my status and Paul's status, because Paul is a household name, which I ain't, and which $99\frac{3}{4}$ per cent of the musicians in the world ain't either."

Denny Laine was evidently less troubled by any wrangles than had been represented in some sections of the rock press. His main concern had centered around contracts. He's a free spirit who dislikes being tied by legal documents. he's suffered too much from too many in the past to enter lightly into any agreement that might limit his movement. "We went to Nashville with the idea that we'd get this group together and we'd all sign contracts and be Wings, as a business thing . . . but then it seemed as if it was being a bit rushed. I thought, 'hang on—let's make sure that this is the right group.' Then I started thinking about contracts, and I decided that I could be in any group without signing a contract . . . It just didn't seem necessary to me, and the minute I said this to Paul he said 'great, that's the way I want it too,' and then I realized that we were only going through this thing with contracts because we'd all been advised to do it. It wasn't what we wanted."

The dust settled and Wings progressed through the rest of the year apparently unruffled. It was, externally, a quiet year for the group. *Junior's Farm/Sally G* was issued (October in UK and November in US) and did respectably, reaching 16 and 3 in the charts of each respective country. (Early the next year, McCartney took the unusual step of flipping the disc, making *Sally G* the A-side. He did it, he said, to give the song a chance of exposure. The record re-entered the US Top 100, reaching 39.)

McCartney had contributed a song—*Mine For Me*— to the Rod Stewart album *Smiler* that was released in the fall of the year. He and Linda went to catch a Faces gig shortly after and found themselves pulled on stage by Rod to join in the song. Paul admitted that the ham in him rose to the occasion and revealed that what one journalist noted as terpsichorean ungainliness was in fact the result of imbibing alcohol. This relaxation seemed to reflect the confidence

SKR

SKR

he now felt with the group and its progress.

This was underlined late in November, 1974 by the long-awaited announcement that Jimmy McCulloch and Geoff Britton were now officially members of Wings. The delay in confirming what everyone already knew was due to contractual problems being ironed-out. These mostly surrounded McCulloch who was signed to Stigwood but may also have sprung from Denny Laine's declared misgivings. A confident Britton told the press: "There was talk of contracts in the beginning, but we decided it was better if nothing was contracted. If you're a real pro and you've got a tour booked, you don't phone up and say, 'I'm not coming.' That's just not on."

Much was made of Britton's accomplishments as a karate expert. He had recently been a member of the British Amateur Karate Association team that had beaten some exponents from Japan—the home of the sport. The victory was recorded on film by director David Litchfield on behalf of McCartney Productions. The resultant 32 minute documentary—*Empty Hand*—was finally released in 1977 with Paul shown on the credits as producer and contributing abstract percussion music—rather ironic as Britton is a drummer!

This was the first movie to emerge from McCartney Productions although several others were mentioned and promised over the years. One—*One Hand Clapping* also directed by Litchfield—was completed and showed the band rehearsing and recording in Nashville. Another was a project involving film of Wings Mark 1 on tour in Europe intercut with animation of three mice who live beneath the stage. That was to be called *The Bruce McMouse Show* and was mentioned intermittently in interviews. Another animated movie was a cherished ambition from Paul's early days as a solo star. One of his first acts after leaving the Beatles was to buy the rights to a newspaper strip featuring Rupert the Bear with the intention of making a cartoon musical. In 1977 he was still asserting he wanted "to make a better film than Walt Disney" but at that time none of the projects had seen the light of day.

With the Wings line-up now publicly stabilized, the group entered 1975 with the prospect of harmonious creativity before them. The first obligation was a new album. Over a year had passed since the release of the last—*Band On The Run*—and it was obvious that they could not afford to delay recording much longer. Paul knew exactly where he wanted to lay this one down—the Sea-Saint Studios in New Orleans. The co-owner is Allen Toussaint, a commanding figure in the New Orleans R & B scene as performer, writer, musician and producer. Among his writing credits are hits like *Ride Your Pony, Working In The Coalmine, Get Out Of My Life Woman* and *Holy Cow* (all for Lee Dorsey) and Ernie K-Doe's *Mother-In-Law*. He's produced a diverse range of talent including Irma Thomas, Clarence 'Frogman' Henry, Dr John and the Meters. What particularly struck Paul's ear was a certain drum sound Toussaint had caught on Labelle's *Lady Marmalade* and he determined to work in Sea-Saint and with Toussaint.

Wings were booked into the studio from the second week in January and set out with high hopes. However, things did not go according to plan. At some point in the stay, a rift appeared in the newly-confirmed line-up as a result of which Geoff Britton was replaced. It's difficult to be certain what exactly precipitated this. Linda later said: "It just didn't jell. It was horrible because we really wanted it to work . . . It was another depressing period. We had started *Venus And Mars* but it just wasn't working."

Two years later, a writer looking back

Drummer Joe English.

EMI

on five years of Wings in *Melody Maker* claimed that there were personality difficulties between Britton and McCulloch because the drummer "hates his guts." Britton told the reporter he'd find out the reasons for his antipathy five minutes after meeting McCulloch. Interestingly, Jimmy had described himself as "a bit weird to get on with at times" during one of the interviews he gave shortly after the official announcement of his and Britton's acceptance into Wings.

He candidly told *Sounds*: "I am a bit weird. Immaturity, I suppose. I've had a lot of experience in music, but experience of life—knowing how to treat people, when to say something and when not to and when you've put your foot in it—I'm still a bit green that way . . . Sometimes there's a Jekyll and Hyde within me. Sometimes I really blow it and get on people's nerves." It is possible that Britton didn't know how to take McCulloch's confused precocity.

Britton's own version of the events, as related to *Melody Maker* nearly two years later, was this: "I was in the States and we were starting work on *Venus And Mars,* and my wife started talking about separation and divorce. I came home to sort it out. Joe English was brought in and I was out. In retrospect, it would have been better to try and keep both things going, but I had to consider that Wings would one day be over and my marriage was a life-long thing."

Geoff said it had "taken me a year to get over leaving Wings" but was obviously putting the best possible face on the whole affair when he remarked: "It's a funny band . . . From a musician's point of view, it's a privilege to do it. From a career point of view, it's madness. No matter how good you are, you're always in the shadow of Paul."

Whether, as many maintain, Britton was pushed or whether, as he says, he jumped out of Wings is immaterial. What mattered at the time was that Paul had a complete album in his head, every detail preordained down to the particular drum sound. (After all, he'd had a year to think about it.) He'd cut three tracks with Britton—*Love In Song, Letting Go* and McCulloch's *Medicine Jar*—and suddenly he had to find a new drummer; the group's third in its short history.

The solution to the crisis came from Tony Dorsey who had been brought in to handle the brass parts on several tracks. (He was later leader of and arranger for the horn section of the Wings roadshow.) He knew of a young drummer of wide experience whom he thought might fit the bill and see the sessions through successfully. The only problem being that he was, at that moment, rehearsing with Bonnie Bramlett, preparatory to going out on tour.

The drummer was Joe English, a native of Rochester, New York (born February 7, 1949) but resident in Geor-

EMI

gia (Dorsey's home state). He answered the call with alacrity (pausing only to arrange a replacement for Bonnie Bramlett's band) and was thrust, unceremoniously, into Wings' frenzied activity. He coped magnificently. He so impressed McCartney that after the completion of the album he was invited to join the band.

Joining Wings was English's turning-point. He had labored long and hard at his profession, paying his dues and serving a gruelling apprenticeship. At the age of 18 he'd joined a band called Jam Factory and through six years had trailed across America on tours, down-bill of rock giants like the Grateful Dead, Janis Joplin and Jimi Hendrix. He'd had plenty of second-hand experience of superstardom, slogged through the grind but reaped none of the rewards. He had plenty of solid, if unspectacular, achievement to look back on—an album for Epic and appearances at America's twin rock meccas, the Fillmores East and West—but an uncertain future.

By about 1973/74 things were looking bleak. Jam Factory broke up and his personal life was shot to hell. As he said, looking back from new-found security in '75, "Two years ago, everything was working against me. My old lady and two kids left me. I had no gigs, no money. I was on the bottom." His only consolation was the unflagging support of his girlfriend, Dayle, who "stuck with me, kept my spirits up, and helped me get through the year." He started doing sessions in the burgeoning Macon music scene that had received such a boost from the success of the Allman Brothers and was expanding fast with the assistance of Phil Walden's Capricorn records. (And, of course, Georgia was about to be put on the map by a thrusting, peanut-growing Governor who had his eyes on bigger things—like the White House!)

Joe English recorded with Wings in New Orleans for the first couple of months of 1975, getting down the tracks that would eventually emerge as *Venus And Mars*. The entourage then headed west to Los Angeles to do the final mixing. (Although, as usual with the McCartneys, it wasn't all work. Their visit to New Orleans coincided with Mardi Gras and, hidden beneath clowns' make-up and costumes, they were able to mingle unobserved in the carnival crowds.)

It was in LA, on the way to Wally Heider's studio for mixing sessions, that Paul turned to Joe in the car and put the proposition to him. After all the difficulties he'd previously encountered finding a suitable drummer, Paul made his mind up fast about English. He was certainly impressed by his musical abilities and, perhaps, swayed by a shared love of the rural life. Just as McCartney—the boy from the terraced streets of Liverpool—relished the role of gentleman farmer and part-time Scottish laird, so city boy Joe English—"I come from the New York ghetto"—had found contentment way down south in Georgia following rustic pursuits. He once described his home environment and it bore strong resemblances to that of Paul and Linda. "We have three dogs, 25 chickens, a goat, six horses, and a cat, Amos, who we brought back from near death after he'd been thrown out of a car. I like to run a Massey Ferguson 150 tractor, fish and plough on the farm. It gets me away from the business."

During their stay in LA the annual Grammy Award ceremony was held. (Grammies are given by the National Academy of Recording Arts and Sciences — NARAS — for "artistic achievement within the recording field, based on artistry in writing, performance, musicianship and engineering." In effect, they are the recording industry's equivalent of Oscars.) Paul and Linda had attended to receive one for the LP *Band On The Run*.

On the Monday following the ceremony—March 3, 1975—Paul, Linda and the three children were driving out of Los Angeles, north along Santa Monica Boulevard, heading back to their temporary base in Malibu. It was just after midnight and Paul had failed to stop at a red light. A highway patrolman flagged down the silver Lincoln Continental and, when he leant through the driving window—presumably to admonish McCartney for his carelessness—his suspicion was aroused by the "strong odor of marijuana." He found, it was later claimed, a smouldering joint on the floor of the car and a quantity of marijuana— reports varied between 16 and 18.5 grammes—in Linda's purse.

Initially, both McCartneys were placed under arrest but Linda insisted that the marijuana was hers alone and she was charged with possession at West Los Angeles police station while Paul was freed and allowed to drive the children home. Linda was detained for two hours before bail was agreed and she was allowed to leave. A spokesman for the police told pressmen: "The whole matter has been put in the hands of the district attorney. It is his decision what charges should be brought in court." There was some speculation at the time that in addition to a charge of possession there might be one for influencing minors as their daughters were present at the time of the incident.

This was the third occasion on which the McCartneys had been involved in

Photo Features International

Capitol

Capitol

David Warner Ellis

Enduring Wings partnership—McCartneys and Laine (right).

drug charges—each time the narcotic was marijuana—and it boded ill for Paul if he was to be charged. He had only recently obtained a visa to work in the States; it had been withheld for some time as a result of the incidents in Sweden and Scotland. John was still fighting the emigration authorities as a result of his conviction seven years previously. There were serious consequences if Paul was involved. While Linda was still a US citizen, Paul was an alien.

The law took its course. In April it was reported that she was being charged with possession (no more was heard of the other charge) and that she was not—as she had at first intended—going to plead not guilty. Instead, she was applying to be put on a police drugs rehabilitation course. An LA police officer explained: "After six months instruction by approved counsellors, first offence drug charges—like that facing Mrs McCartney—are usually dropped."

In May came the news that Judge Brian Cuhan had offered Linda the alternative of having psychiatric treatment or standing trial. She had opted for the former and the judge had ordered that she attend six sessions with a psychiatrist. He allowed her to follow this course in London, where she and Paul had returned with the children. In November, some newspapers carried short agency reports stating: "Linda McCartney . . . has had a charge of possessing marijuana dismissed by a Los Angeles court because she completed a six-month course in England on the danger of drugs."

Yet again, the McCartneys had been dealt with leniently. But the fact remained that they had been busted three times in as many years. They seemed to be subject to more than usual police activity. Paul was asked later that year by *New Musical Express* whether he thought they were "being got at." "No. I don't at all . . . It's just one of those things. Just the luck of the draw. I don't think it mounts up to any kind of conspiracy . . . The only really unfortunate thing about it is that it starts to get you a reputation as a kind of druggie. It is really only a minor offence. It isn't something we take too seriously, and of course the press image is really far worse.

"We're not serious drug addicts or anything. We just try to keep it quiet and not get into it a lot, because even talking about it . . . is like adding to it . . . The fact is it's illegal, and if a thing's illegal you're liable to get caught doing it."

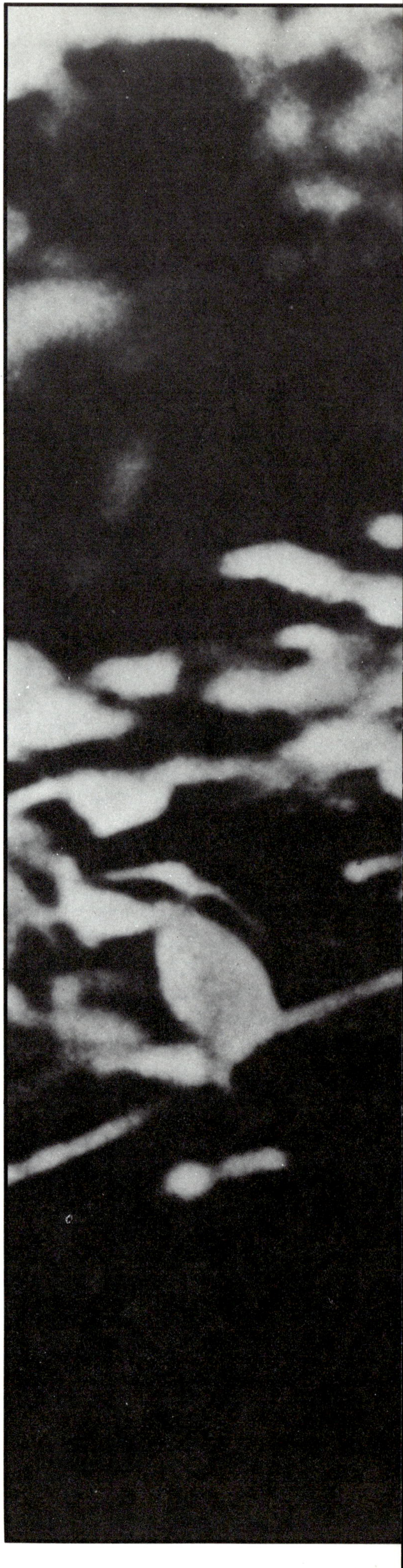

Capitol

EMI

WINGS ACROSS THE WORLD

McCartney Productions

The most important musical event for Wings in 1975 was the release of the new album that could truthfully be described as long-awaited. By the time it hit the record stores in May the gap since *Band On The Run* had stretched to very nearly 18 months. Now, at last, came *Venus And Mars*.

It was mostly greeted with approval, although it was almost universally felt to be softer and less incisive than *Band On The Run*. It was the usual McCartney mélange of styles, influences and moods and critics were sometimes at a loss to know why excellent rock numbers like *Letting Go* and *Listen To What The Man Said* should be bracketed with a camp Astaire-styled pastiche like *You Gave Me The Answer* (which was a further expression of McCartney nostalgia in the vein of *Honey Pie* or *Your Mother Should Know*). The use of fragments and reprises was incorporated again (notably the title song kicking off both sides and the segue of *Treat Her Gently* into *Lonely Old People*).

What really infuriated some British critics was the final track. It was a version of the theme from the immensely popular afternoon TV soap opera, *Crossroads*. And it seemed to confirm in the minds of all his detractors McCartney's pandering to popular taste (or even bad, semi-moronic taste, as some would castigate); here was proof positive that McCartney was a light-weight pop musician of no value or significance. One British journalist levelled a crushing barrage against McCartney and the album. Describing *Venus And Mars* as "one of the worst albums I've ever heard from a so-called 'Major artist'," he launched into the attack. He asserted that until *Band On The Run* the "prevailing assessment" of McCartney was that he "was the possessor of a 'basically bourgeois talent'—which meant that he was essentially uncommitted to rock & roll, was irremedially cutesy-pie . . . wrote songs that begged for Andy Williams to cover them . . . allowed an overwhelming facility for pleasant melody and easy-going charm to degenerate into vacuous glibness, angled his music at the mums and dads, came off poorly in comparison to the gritty honesty and commitment of John Lennon."

The fulcrum of that attack lies in the phrase "essentially uncommitted to rock & roll." Time and again this has been hurled at him. It is as if he has betrayed a sacred trust; frittered away his potential; settled for easy-listening pap rather than breaking new ground and pushing the frontiers of rock forward. It was said that he had deserted the "qualities which one could quite reasonably demand from the work of an artist of Paul McCartney's eminence" and replaced them with "a vapid, shallow prettiness which is ultimately more saddening than the work of even the dumbest no-hoper."

TV ad for Venus And Mars LP.

McCartney Productions

This is demonstrably untrue; McCartney *is* a major talent and influence. The cry of anguish of these rock pundits springs mainly from the fact that Paul is, after all, an ex-Beatle; one quarter of the greatest rock group the world has ever seen and one half of the most successful, experimental, creative, barrier-busting songwriting team in the history of rock (and, some would say, all popular music). "He could be so good!" they howl. "If only he was *committed* to rock & roll." But as Linda once said, "Paul isn't God. The Beatles were not Gods." One of the advantages of his independence from the collective responsibility of the Beatles was that he could do what he wanted and not what others expected of him. This boy was *not* "gonna carry that weight a long time."

Although wounded by them, McCartney shrugs at such outbursts. He's heard them so many times before and he's too old a hand to be pressured into doing what others want. He will explain, patiently, that he included the theme from *Crossroads* because the previous song on the album—*Lonely Old People*—was about the emptiness and isolation of old age. His elderly couple are forgotten husks, excluded from the bustling activity around them. Life holds little for them, except to wander dispiritedly back into the old people's home and be swept up in the daily dramas of other people's lives—the lives of the characters in a TV serial.

The tune holds no relevance to anyone outside Britain. To those who've never seen *Crossroads,* its theme is simply a pleasant melody. As McCartney told his critic on *New Musical Express:* "The fellow who was helping me arrange this stuff [Tony Dorsey] . . . thought it was just a lovely tune. He thought I'd written it. He thought it was just a beautiful little tune, and it is." McCartney used it because "it fitted." As simple as that. That the TV company adopted his arrangement brought him pleasure because everyone likes to have their work recognized and caused more apoplexy among the guardians of rock's 'purity'.

One weighty British newspaper warned its readers "beware McCartney's love of suburbia," claimed that since his break with Lennon "his music has developed into facile lightness" and found the fact that he had recorded *Crossroads* "heart-chilling"! McCartney sees it as no more surprising than recording *Mary Had A Little Lamb* shortly after *Give Ireland Back To The Irish.* He acknowledges his facility in songwriting and is delighted to have it. He has, only half-mockingly, described himself as "a hack" because he can knock off *Live And Let Die* to order. He refuses to analyze his role in and contribution to rock music. He just gets on with the job and occasionally, unashamedly, allows the ham in him, the sentimental, even mawkish side, to show through.

Venus And Mars received some harsh

EMI

and, on the whole, unfair criticism. It was a less considerable album than *Band On The Run*, a fact recognized by McCartney, but it was still full of good things not least of them *Listen To What The Man Said*. As a single this hit number 1 in the States (as did the album), the eighth Wings single in succession to make the Top 10.

There had been a long gap between albums and a greater one since Wings had toured. Once again McCartney had to discover whether the new line-up that worked well in the studio could repeat its success on the road. Both Jimmy McCulloch and Joe English were untried in Wings' concerts.

McCartney wanted to take the band round Britain again, to get it right for the home audiences (who had seen the nucleus of the group before and had some point of comparison) before spreading his Wings and migrating towards new territories, especially America. Being a methodical man (and a perfectionist) he called for a series of long and comprehensive rehearsals at which every element of the roadshow would be brought together to practice the roles he would demand of them nightly.

This was to be a far bigger, more complex affair than his previous, rather informal, excursions. As a result of the *Venus And Mars* sessions he was using a horn section to back-up and add body to the group. He brought in Tony Dorsey as 'head wrangler' to lead, organize and arrange the horns. Dorsey recruited two of New Orleans' top brass players—Steve Howard on trumpet and flugelhorn and Thaddeus Richard, a multi-instrumentalist who specialized in saxophone, clarinet and flute. The fourth member was a throwback to McCartney's past.

Howie Casey is a Liverpudlian musician whose career goes back to the early days of rock & roll. He had trodden the same tough road as the Beatles before their success. He'd played around the city and been among the first to venture across the North Sea to the thriving scene in Hamburg. (Herein lies a nice irony. In his book *The Man Who Gave The Beatles Away*—Coronet—the Beatles' first manager, Allan Williams, recounts how he wrote to Howie, then with Derry and the Seniors, telling him to expect the arrival of the Beatles. In return he received a letter that, with expletives deleted, said in effect: "Look, man, we've got a great . . . scene going here in Hamburg. Now you want to . . . it up by sending over that bum group, the Beatles. They're no . . . good. We don't want them here and they will be bad for the scene. If you want to send another group, why not Rory Storm and the Hurricanes? A . . . good group . . . Don't send the . . . Beatles."!)

Derry and the Seniors may have been a good band (they were among the first—if not the very first—Liverpool groups to release a disc, in 1961) but they failed to do as well as the despised Beatles. They split and Howie played with a succession of bands with varying success until he decided to turn his prowess as a saxophonist to use as a sessionman. In this capacity he was hired to play on *Band On The Run*. Any disputes in the past between bands were forgotton, Casey was welcomed to the fold, spoke highly of his Wing commander and fitted snugly into the backup.

EMI

To muster all the personnel and thoroughly rehearse all the hardware that modern rock roadshows require, McCartney called a series of long sessions in a massive sound-stage on the lot of the EMI movie studios in London. Here the musicians, road crew, lighting and sound men and assorted technical wizards gathered for exhaustive—and exhausting—run-throughs. The idea was to iron out as many problems—both evident and potential—and foresee as many contingencies and snags as possible. McCartney was a demanding, meticulous taskmaster; he made everyone go over and over the long performance until it was clockwork efficient and note perfect. He held a full dress rehearsal in front of a knowledgeable and scrutinous audience of record industry notables. This showed up a few edges that needed smoothing and, after last minute polishing, the circus—nearly 50 people, with over 12 tons of equipment, a dozen or more guitars, six keyboard instruments and the other accoutrements necessary to entertain fans in the '70s—lumbered on to the roads of Britain.

This was a comparatively short tour, only 12 British cities spread over two weeks but the first show at the Southampton Gaumont on September 9, 1975 was the curtain raiser for a 13-month, 10-nation tour across the world, playing nearly 80 concerts along the way. Only three years previously, on the University jaunt of 1972, Wings had flapped; in Europe the same year they'd flown; on the first full British tour of '73 they were soaring; by the end of this mammoth progress Wings would be strato-cruising.

From the reviews of that first gig and the hundreds that followed all through the next year, it was evident that Wings had established themselves as one of the foremost outfits in '70s rock. The British tour was generally welcomed in the rock press as excellent though nearly every notice had a percentage of criticism. The most extreme example was in the scrupulous *Melody Maker* that ran the opinions of two reviewers in an effort to achieve balance. In one the editor described a London concert as "vapid . . . a lackluster performance . . . nothing will shake my conviction that [the audience] were applauding an ex-Beatle's appearance rather than the Wings concert. For there are equally good rock shows on in most cities all the time; but a real live Beatle? That's rarity value."

To his credit, the editor very fairly offered equal space to one of his staff who thought the concert "Excellent from all points of view," was unstinting in his praise of the band (he even had a good word for Linda—one of the most abused performers in rock—saying her "keyboard playing is more than adequate for the fills she is called upon to produce") and concluded that the show fell just short of perfection.

Wings offered their increasingly enthusiastic audiences a non-stop two-hour show (uncluttered with support acts) of about 30 numbers. The four up-front members swapped instruments in a dazzling show of versatility and everyone had a chance to handle either a song (McCulloch on *Medicine Jar,* Laine on *Go Now!*) or an instrumental solo. Spliced into the middle of the set was a much-applauded acoustic section, the undoubted high-point of which was Paul's rendition of *I've Just Seen A Face, Blackbird* and *Yesterday.* These, together with *Lady Madonna* and *The Long And Winding Road* elsewhere in the show, were his first live acknowledgement of his Beatle past. A reconciliation with his previous persona.

The whole evening was a brilliant exercise in crowd pleasing from a man who had been entertaining audiences for half his life. His attitude towards it was simple: "I like music and we are in very depressed times, so if the music cheers people up that must be good." And he was determined to appeal across as broad an age spectrum as possible. Wings pulled in the teen fans who dimly realized that Paul had been in a group before as well as those—some now parents—who felt their first stirrings of adolescent excitement to the strains of *She Loves You* and *Please Please Me.* "Age does not make any difference as far as our fans are concerned—even in the Beatle days we had older fans. Our aim is that everyone should like us," Paul declared.

The success of the British concerts must have confirmed McCartney's opinion that—after several tries and many disappointments—he'd got the mix right at last. Within his disciplined set-up Jimmy McCulloch—previously noted as a free-ranging guitarist who occasionally over-indulged his love of jamming—was able to play beautifully-controlled lead and take his place in the front line. At the back, Joe English laid down a firm rhythmic base upon which the others built.

Linda spoke admiringly of the band on this tour, telling *Melody Maker*: "Paul didn't feel confidence in the band before, whereas this band, he really knows he can get up there and sing. Because he knows that everybody else knows what they're doing . . . With this, we've listened to it and criticized it . . . Denny has been with us always, and he'd always fit in . . . Henry didn't really fit in. Jimmy is great and I think he'll improve a lot, he'll get better and better and really get his own style. And Joe English is a very good drummer, who has never really done anything big before. He's great on rhythms, and he doesn't come on like 'I'm a great drummer.' He just gets behind it. . . . You can't ever say what's going to be in the future, but I'd like to see this band carry on."

Secure in the knowledge that the band and the show were world-beaters, Paul started thinking in earnest about going out and beating the world. He had always kept America as his ultimate goal and now, with visa problems cleared up and a stable group, it became a reality. But there were other fields to conquer first. There was a clamoring from the East, particularly Japan and Australia, to see the group and so, after a short break to catch breath, they set off for a tour of the Antipodes during the first two weeks of November.

Australia had given the Beatles some of the most riotous, hysterical welcomes in the '60s and very nearly repeated them for Wings. The tour of five major cities was a triumphant sell-out, exceeding all

EMI

Capitol

Capitol

SILLY LOVE

EMI

expectation. Or, as Paul rather laconically put it: "We had fab fun . . . The audiences were great and we just dug playing. It was more like a holiday." Some holiday. So great was the demand for tickets that scalpers were asking, and getting, in Paul's phrase, "Sinatra prices" for seats.

The only pall thrown over the success was the attitude of the Japanese government. It banned the group from entry because of McCartney's drug conviction. Paul explained it to *Melody Maker*: "It was the Minister of Justice's fault. I suppose he'd say it was my fault for having smoked some of the deadly weed. But we had our visas signed by the London Japanese Embassy. Everything had been cleared . . . and we were in Australia, just about a week out from going to Japan when a little note arrived saying the Japanese Minister of Justice says 'No' . . . It was just one of those things but we felt a bit sick about it."

Due to the incredible demand for tickets in Australia, Wings did a TV show there "for all the people who couldn't get in to see us." As soon as he heard about the ban, he had a print of the show struck and sent to Japan. It was shown on TV there—so fans weren't entirely disappointed—together with a long programme added on to it in which the merits and demerits of marijuana were discussed. The latter didn't entirely please McCartney who said "In a way we became martyrs for the cause, which is a drag."

After Australia—the first, and hugely successful, test outside Wings' familiar European stamping grounds—and before the run-up to America, the group retired to the studios to work on an album. McCartney had thought about and planned it in the last months of 1975 (a good opportunity for reflection presented itself when Japan was cancelled and he holidayed in Hawaii instead) and had worked out some very definite ideas. He felt that the group had reached the point at which he could emphasize its unity; bring home to the public that Wings was a group in every sense of the word. He wanted to make this a *group* album with everyone getting a chance to show what they could do. And to buttress the point, the band was no longer styled 'Paul McCartney and Wings'. He felt when releasing *Venus And Mars* (the first album since *Wildlife* not to carry his name prominently) that giving the group a supporting credit was "an embarrassment to me. It was never Paul McCartney and the Beatles, Paul McCartney and the Quarrymen, or Paul McCartney and the Moondogs. [The latter two being names tried and dropped before 'Beatles' was adopted.] Wings is quicker and easier to say and everybody knows I'm in the group anyway."

Wings At The Speed Of Sound was the group's first truly democratic album. It included songs written and performed by Jimmy McCulloch and Denny Laine

EMI

(*Wino Junko* and *Time To Hide* respectively) as well as three McCartney songs handed out to the others to sing—*Cook Of The House* for Linda, *The Note You Never Wrote* for Denny and *Must Do Something About It*, Joe English's debut as a vocalist. Even the brass section was allowed its head on *Silly Love Songs*, the musicians working out their parts and, Paul commented, "they can really get behind it because it's their bit."

The record really split the critics into two camps. For example, one felt that English "unleashes a really professional soul sound." (Paul agreed: "He can sing well... but it's nothing to what he *could* do.") But another maintained "it's crazy to have other people sing your songs when you can sing them so much better yourself. It's just about understandable letting the wife sing a track . . . but to have drummer Joe English and Laine have a go is simply not on when they're so obviously inferior singers to Paul himself."

While many felt that *Speed Of Sound* was a pleasant album with occasional delights but not a major McCartney work, some were not so kind. One said "McCartney has made another duff elpee" and another asserted, more in sorrow than in anger, that it was "a major disappointment," a "predictable drone" containing "rocking-chair music." Notwithstanding such comment, the album shot to number 1 in America and quickly went platinum (indicating a sale of 1,000,000 in the US) and the hugely-successful single from it—*Silly Love Songs*—was the biggest selling single of the year there. A second single—*Let 'Em In*—gleaned gold for sales of over a million. McCartney may have been stung by some of the criticism but he could console himself that the mighty sales augured extremely well for his biggest challenge yet—the flight across, and hopefully conquest of, America.

Before launching themselves upon their most important campaign yet, Wings flipped over to the Continent to play four countries in a week during March and returned to base to plan the assault on the States. Wings Over America—as the tour was dubbed—was to stretch through May and June 1976, taking in 19 cities plus Toronto, Canada. (It was originally scheduled for April and May but Jimmy McCulloch fell after the last concert in Paris and broke the little finger of his left hand, forcing a postponement.)

To describe the Wings tour of the States as a campaign is not entirely fanciful. Paul McCartney is a strategist. He had planned each phase carefully and logically. Everything was building towards the US because he recognized: "America *is* the . . . biggest place on earth that you can go to play, outside of China and Russia . . . America is the biggie, there's no doubt about that." And there were very good reasons why he had, in short order, played Britain, Australia and then Europe before embarking on America.

He expounded his tactical theories to *Sounds*: "It would have been silly to do it the other way around, to come into your biggest halls . . . I mean, to play 20,000 people you've got to have it together. About 14,000 was the top we played in Australia. In England, you see, you can play certain special halls, but the normal venues are like 3000 . . . So very naturally we started off with 3000 people, and then we went to 5000, 6000, 14,000 in Australia, and then we played some bigger halls in Europe, which were more towards 15,000 . . . I like things like that. I like things step by step."

Such care and thought is typical of all his forward thinking. He recalled the receptions the Beatles received 10 years previously—so hysterical that nothing was audible to those who had actually come to listen and not to scream. Consequently he demanded the very best sound system that modern technology could provide. It wasn't that he was expecting Beatle-type screaming and needed to be able to drown it—although overcoming audience noise was one consideration—so much as a desire to please. "Hopefully, even the people right at the back . . . can hear exactly what we're doing, the little nuances."

His perfectionism drove him to arrive at each venue early enough to undertake a full sound check prior to every concert and conduct a short post mortem with the technicians at the end of the evening. Such attention to detail paid off and reviewers often congratulated Wings on the clarity and precision of their sound quality.

However hard he worked at the minutiae of the tour, Paul could not guarantee success. The specter of failure always hovers in a corner of the mind and you cannot plan away your nerves. Shortly before setting out, Paul and Linda talked to Hunter Davies (who had written the Beatles' official biography) of the London *Sunday Times.* They both spoke of their fears. Paul's centered around the attitude of the press. "They now seem to like us, at least in Britain they do. I know in America the press will be sitting in the front three rows, their pencils ready." But he felt confident enough to face his judges with equanimity. "It doesn't really matter what they say. I'm not as precious about Wings as I used to be. If it folds, it folds, hard luck. I'll be very upset. I'll say 'Sod it,' but we'll survive. I feel very secure with Wings now."

Linda, who was going home as a star for the first time and didn't have half a lifetime of performing experience behind her, found it hard to be as philosophical as her husband: "What worries me most about America is that we'll have to start again . . . I'll obviously be criticized and I'll hate it. I'd love to put the critics up on stage and see them do better. You lose a few years of your life on stage. You live on your adrenalin . . . I don't want to spend my life touring."

In the event, the worries were unnecessary. From the first concert in Fort Worth, Texas on May 3, 1976, America opened its heart to Wings. McCARTNEY'S TOUR STARTS TRIUMPHANTLY proclaimed *The New York Times* and *The Los Angeles Times* agreed: McCARTNEY, WINGS SOAR IN TEXAS. Everywhere Wings went the press redounded with praise. "Paul McCartney can rest easy. His place as one of the greatest rock & rollers of all time is assured," trumpeted *The Washington Post* and considered the show to be "an almost ideal display of what live rock & roll should be . . . as exciting visually as it was musically."

Such laudatory notices were repeated across the continent. The press adjectives were enforced—rather more solidly—by the unemotional statistics that appeared after the tour: nearly 600,000 people paid to see the band (snapping up the tickets so fast that records were set for sell-out speeds); 67,100 turned up at the Seattle Kingdome, a world indoor concert attendance record for one performance by a single act; $336,000 grossed in Philadelphia making one of the biggest rock box office receipts of the year. After every performance, McCartney set aside time to see the press. As a result his record company was able to boast: "Wings generated more press coverage in 1976 than any other Capitol artist and probably more than virtually any musical entity in the world."

McCartney was understandably exul-

EMI

EMI

tant. This was his vindication. He had returned to the scene of the Beatles' greatest triumphs—exactly 10 years after their last concert in San Francisco and with the pinnacle of Shea Stadium ever in his mind—and scored a memorable victory. He was unquestionably the most successful ex-Beatle, indisputably one of the major rock figures in the '70s. The impact should not be underrated. As the *Los Angeles Times* said in connection with the debut at Fort Worth: "When the house lights dimmed . . . virtually everyone in the arena stood in anticipation of what was clearly the most notable return to rock concerts since Bob Dylan's 1974 appearance in Chicago."

The star was rather breath-taken by the extent of the success. "In 10 years, I'll be looking back and remembering everything about it. At the moment, I'm just zooming through it all . . . If I were able to get away from the tour for a while and come back to it through some sort of time machine, I'd definitely be freaking out. I'd be going 'Wow. This is great.' Occasionally, on the plane, we'll get the group together and say 'Oh great, isn't it?' But most of the time, it's hard to see what is really happening until you get away from it . . .

"That's what I love about life: its inexactness. After the Beatles, you would have thought it would have been pretty much impossible for me to follow that and to get anything else going. At least, I thought that. But life is inexact. It doesn't work according to plan. This tour has convinced us that we're a group and I think it has convinced audiences, too. This wasn't just a one-time trip. This is going to be a working band. We'll be back."

Wings Over America was everything McCartney had hoped for—and much more. Having carried all before them, Wings would have been excused for wanting to rest for a while. But that was not McCartney's intention. No sooner had they returned home from America than he was planning another swift sweep through Europe culminating in three mammoth concerts at London's Empire Pool, Wembley—the conquering heroes being accorded their laurels by an adoring public.

Before launching themselves on this lap of honor, Paul announced that he was designating a Buddy Holly week to be held during early September. To celebrate the event, Denny Laine issued a single of Holly's *It's So Easy/Listen To Me* (a prelude to an album, *Holly Days*, produced by Paul and to be released at a later date) and the climax was to be a very exclusive lunch hosted by the McCartneys for numerous rock luminaries including Elton John, Eric Clapton and Roger Daltry. Also present was Holly's producer and co-writer Norman Petty who presented Paul with a rather grisly gift—the cufflinks Holly was wearing when his plane crashed and which had been salvaged from the

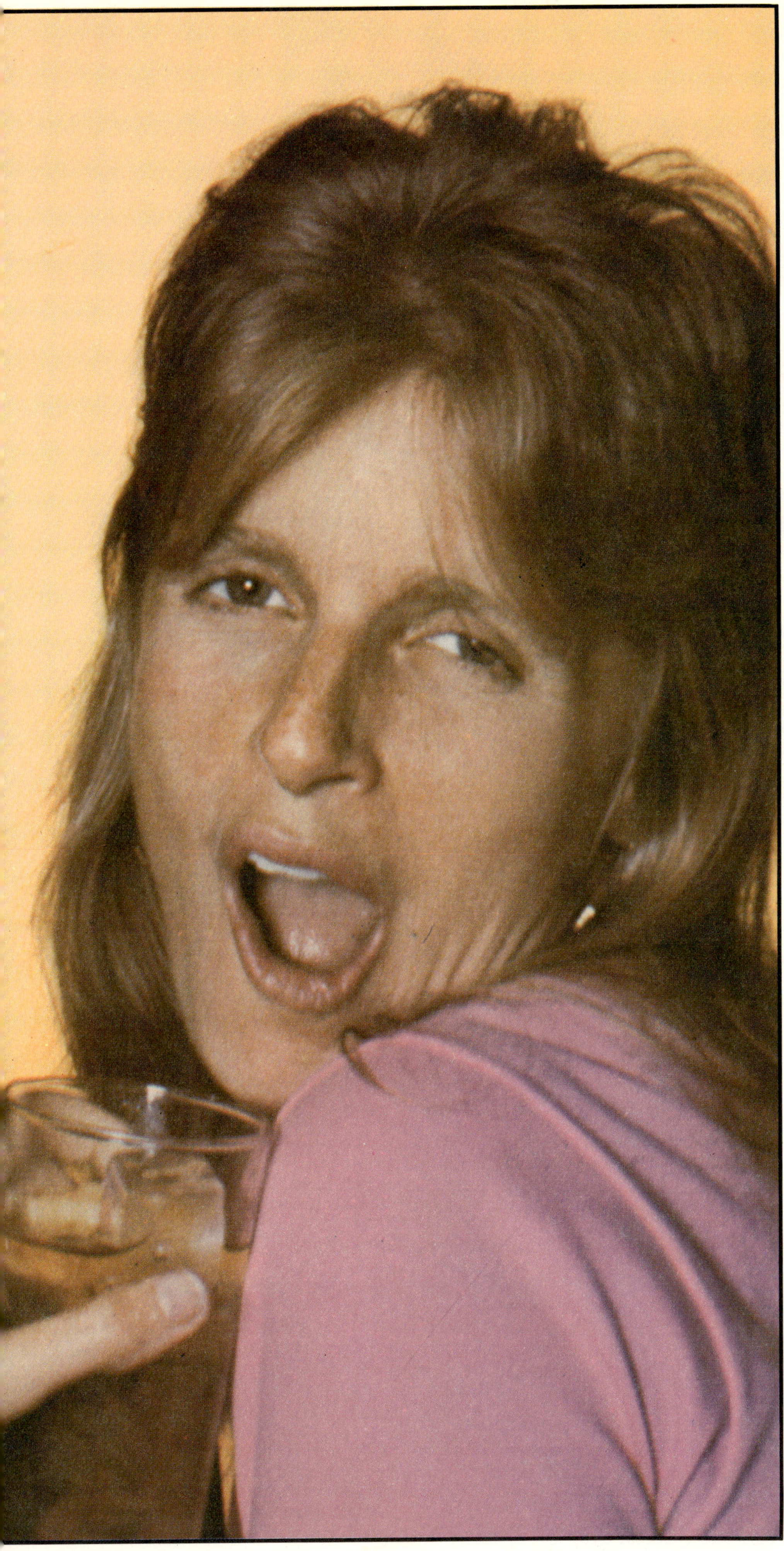

Camera Press

wreckage. While these events sprang from a genuine regard and affection for the memory of one of rock's greats, they perhaps weren't entirely altruistic. The shrewd Mr McCartney had made a canny business move in 1971 when he purchased the Buddy Holly publishing catalogue, giving him the copyright in such enduring hits as *That'll Be The Day*, *Peggy Sue* and *Not Fade Away*.

Paul seemed to be constantly headline-grabbing in that remarkable summer of '76—Britain's hottest and most arid in living memory. When the details of the group's mini-tour of the Continent were unveiled it was revealed that in addition to playing Vienna (Austria), Zagreb (Jugoslavia; hailed as the first concert "by a really major rock band in a communist country." Wings also breached the Iron Curtain when *Band On The Run* was the first rock album to gain official release in Russia) and Munich (Germany) the group would be playing a vast charity concert in St Mark's Square, Venice.

This was arranged by the United Nations Educational, Scientific and Cultural Organization (UNESCO) to focus attention on the desperate need to raise funds for the restoration of Venice which—due to years of neglect and inundation—was gradually but steadily sinking back into the waters that it had once dominated. A week of concerts had been arranged and artists contributing included Peter Ustinov, Ravi Shankar and Mort Shuman. The authorities wanted to interest young people in the glorious city's fate and approached Wings who instantly—and at rather short notice—agreed to appear. McCartney generously offered to pay for transport and equipment and to give their services free while the organizing committee would foot the bill for hotels, erecting the stage and seating in the Piazza. To help pay for his considerable investment, McCartney hurriedly arranged the gigs in the other three cities. It was hoped to take approximately £54,000 of which, it was estimated, £25,000 would go to the preservation fund after expenses. The primary object, however, was to put Venice in the center of the world stage.

This was achieved. The media flocked to the city from all over the world (and noted, a trifle gleefully, that the trucks carrying sound equipment to help save the fabric of Venice were so heavy they actually cracked some ancient paving flags!) The historic Piazza San Marco had been zoned to allow a maximum audience of 15,000 people—some paying £10 for their seats—but on the night the hordes overwhelmed the security guards and about twice that number crammed into the square. They were entertained by a tremendous show—not only musically but visually because Wings' lighting crew utilized the beautiful setting to the very best effect. Venice got its publicity and Wings didn't do too badly out of it either.

EMI

One of the biggest events in London's '76 rock calendar was Wings' swoop on London at the Empire Pool, Wembley. (The other big one had been the Rolling Stones in May which was generally adjudged a failure—albeit an honorable one.) After so much praise, so many eulogies, such free use of plauditory adjectives, it was inevitable that there would be something of a critical backlash. Perhaps the rock reviewers were becoming jaded, because they tended to be disagreeable and picky. They were, however, out of step with public opinion (isn't that often the case?) The three shows were held by many who saw them to be among the most satisfying and imaginative they had ever witnessed. While the rock media grumbled, the paying customers applauded vigorously and would undoubtedly have packed the cavernous, unsuitable hall every night for another week, given the chance.

Wings' incredible year slowly wound down but it wasn't over yet, at least not for the McCartneys. In November came news of yet another film project, a science fiction musical in which the group would act and perform. It was the result of a meeting between the group and Gene Roddenberry, the producer of TV's cult show *Star Trek*. In December, Linda—now being fully accepted, even by the most acid of commentators, as an integral part of Wings—displayed her other talent, that of the successful photographer. A glossy, fat book of her work—*Linda's Pictures*—was issued, containing a wide selection of her work from the earliest Rolling Stones session in New York, through her days at the Fillmore East (where she shot many of the '60s greats) to a large portfolio devoted to Paul and the family.

It's typical of her gutsiness that, having just weathered years of stinging criticism, she offered herself up yet again to be shied at by the carpers. It is to her credit that the reviews were mostly excellent. There is no greater praise than that which comes from a successful professional; Terry O'Neill is probably the foremost photographer of stars and glamor subjects, the man most trusted by beautiful women and top rock and movie people to shoot accurately and well. He reviewed *Linda's Pictures* in *Melody Maker:* "I fully expected this book to be an unmitigated disaster. However, I was very pleasantly surprised and can only take my hat off as one professional to another. Well done! . . . Very few good photographers emerge from the rock world and against that criterion, she has done more than well . . . Her work of her husband and family is simply excellent; she tells a story with every shot . . ."

The group rounded off a memorable year with the release of the enormous triple album, *Wings Over America*. It was, in every sense of the word, a record of the momentous US tour. Nearly every one of the 34 concerts was taped; later McCartney and engineers listened to this huge bulk of material, establishing the five best versions of the 28 songs to be included. Then Paul set himself the laborious task of selecting the finest of these. He is reported to have devoted up to 14 hours a day, seven days a week for six weeks in the selection, mixing and mastering of *Wings Over America*.

The time was well spent. Most reviewers were generous in their praise, some hailed it is as a masterpiece, a few complained that it should have been reduced to four sides. The public didn't quibble, it slapped down the hefty asking price and agreed with one reviewer who bravely proclaimed it as an invaluable recording of "the best rock band in the world, at their best."

As Paul McCartney entered the last quarter of the twentieth century—a century upon which he had made his mark—he had every reason to be satisfied with his achievements. Professionally, he was one of the best known young men in the world (a newspaper which ran his 'Memoirs' for three days in 1977 called him "the world's greatest pop musician" and "The Grand Young Man of pop"!) He was rich. Although not as rich as some might believe, and certainly not as rich as a man who—singly or in partnership—was probably responsible for more hits than anyone else in the history of popular music might expect to be. Or as an ex-member of the biggest selling group ever, could be. (By 1977, *The Guinness Book Of Records* maintained that the Beatles had sold the equivalent of 545,000,000 singles, world-wide. This is computed by counting albums as six singles units. It was estimated that the group had sold 85,000,000 albums in all.)

Paul McCartney had also managed a further remarkable feat. He had repeated his success. He had created a second supergroup. Wings would never equal the success of the Beatles (would any group?) but under Paul's careful command, in a few short years it was big enough to rate as one of the most popular and successful bands in the world. The easiest way to measure success is by statistics (although these cannot convey the influence a band exerts, the impact it has on its audience, the loyalty and fanaticism it commands or the excitement it generates). By 1977, figures were appearing to support the claim that Wings were world-beaters. *Wings Over America* was the first triple album by any band to go to number 1 in the States. (Only two other triples had ever made it—*Woodstock* and George Harrison's *All Things Must Pass*.) Over the years, McCartney and Wings had received seven gold singles (denoting million sales), eight gold albums (denoting sales of half-a-million), six platinum albums (denoting million sales) and three double platinum albums.

In 1976 alone the group had received a platinum record as well as a gold for *Speed Of Sound* (and the Beatles compilation *Rock 'N' Roll Music* went platinum as well) and gold discs for *Silly Love Songs* and *Let 'Em In*. Furthermore, *Silly Love Songs* headed *Variety*'s and *Billboard*'s list of the 100 Best-Selling Pop Singles of 1976. (*Let 'Em In* was 25th and 67th respectively.)

By his own admission, in the years 1974–76 McCartney "earned more money than I have ever earned in all the other so-called boom years put together." As he told the *Daily Express*, rather ruefully, "We were supposed to have sold 300,000,000 records. [The actual figures, are as we have seen, higher.] If you compute that and say the group should have had 10p a go, then where did that money go?"

After he had finally extricated himself from all his unwanted legal entanglements, he was a wiser man. He never made the same mistakes again. If he wrote a song, he made sure he owned it, that every penny generated by it came into the coffers of his own company. This lesson was hard learnt after seeing *Yesterday* slip out of his grasp. It has

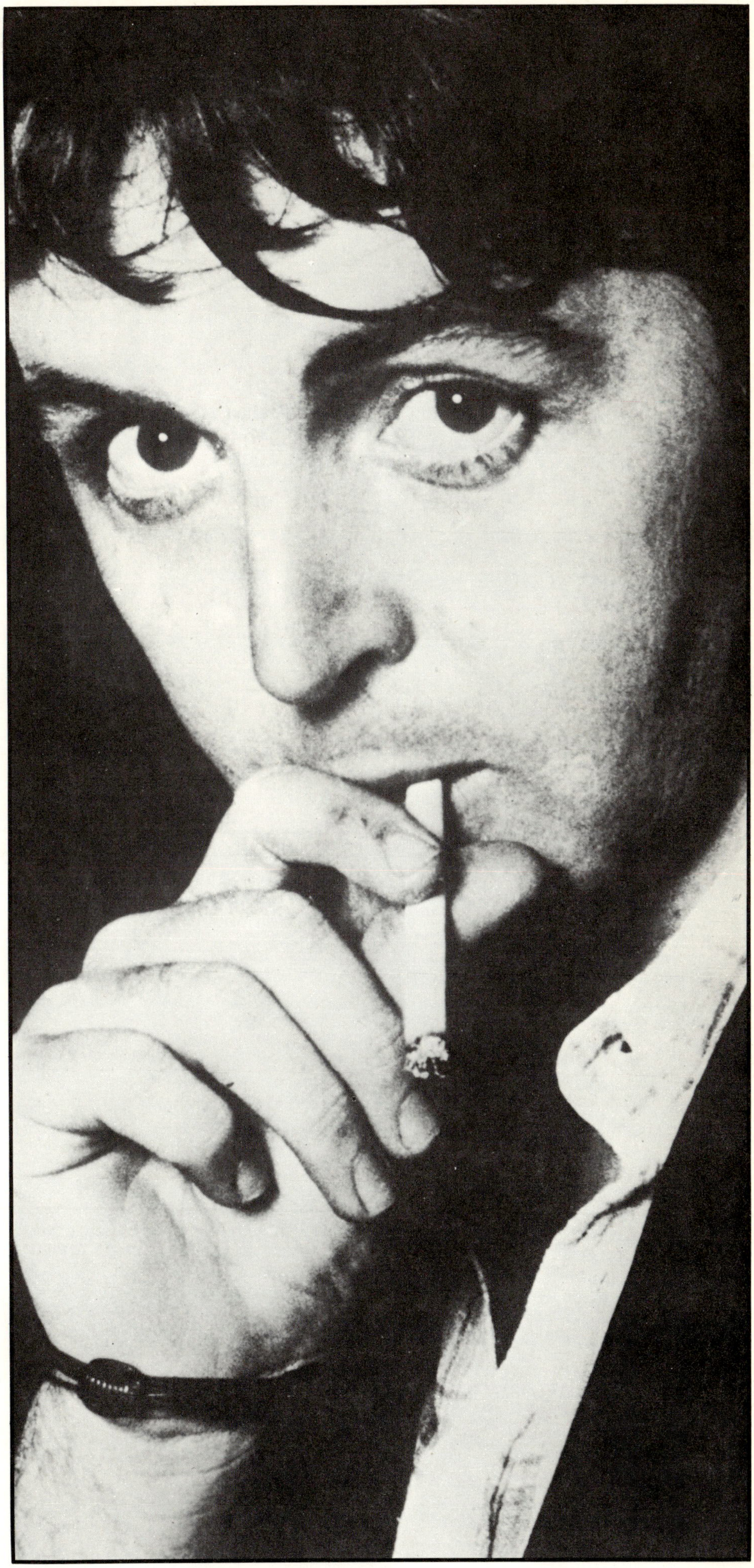

Capitol

Capitol

been reckoned there are 1200 versions of the song, all earning enough to keep the copyright holder comfortably for the rest of his life. McCartney has acknowledged that *Yesterday* is "probably the only big song I did on my own." But the song is owned by Lord Grade. Paul doesn't begrudge him that—"he's a good businessman and he heard it was up for sale"—but never again will he let a goldmine drift away.

As he entered his mid-thirties, Paul McCartney was, from all the evidence, a happy man. Professional success is one thing (and certainly to be desired) but he had achieved something more. With Linda—and despite the gloomy prophecy of self-styled friends—he found a contentment and security that few rock stars know. His marriage and his family were central to his life. He cherished the stability and warmth they afforded. And he was in the enviable position of being able to combine his family AND his career. He went nowhere without the children and he suspended all touring during 1977 because Linda was expecting their third baby in September. (If a boy it was to be called James after his father and, indeed, himself.)

He was not embarrassed to declare how important the family was to him. "Linda and I know everyone says marriage is old-fashioned. We know the contract is just a piece of paper," he told a newspaper. "But it's up to you what you make out of that piece of paper. I'm really happy with the blonde lady. These days it's my family that's my world. I've discovered I'm rather old-fashioned. I believe in the contract. And I feel it is very important to my children that they have a proper mother and father. Our children and our life together will always come first. Because no matter how much money one has . . . well, without happiness it means nothing."

He realized this rather cosy new role was in sharp contrast to the hell-raising young bachelor of earlier years. As he told the *Daily Mail*: "My lifestyle today and my attitude towards everything is very different from the '60s when the Beatles were the whole bit. I really had a wild time in my early days, especially when we first toured America in 1964. But I have told Linda everything. I have no secrets from her. I had the time of my life then in many ways but, honestly, with my family and everything I am much happier now."

He was the last of the Beatles to marry and this perhaps helped him to get his life into perspective. He had had a long relationship with actress Jane Asher, lasting through many of the Beatles most successful years and there were constant rumors that they would eventually marry. Indeed, in December, 1967, Paul had said quite emphatically: "We shall get married . . . I think everyone knows this. But when we don't know." In the event they did not wed. In May, '68 Paul had renewed his friendship with Linda in New York and by July

LFI

Jane Asher said on television that the engagement was off.

His lengthy relationship with Jane Asher might be considered a surrogate marriage and as such it ended with none of the matrimonial complications surrounding the other Beatles. John's marriage to Cynthia ended when he left her for Yoko; Ringo—always considered the steadiest and most 'family' of the Beatles—divorced Maureen; Patti Boyd left George Harrison for Eric Clapton. Ironically, the most eligible bachelor settled most readily into wedded life.

The McCartneys' family life has two main bases—the rambling Georgian house in St John's Wood, London and the two-farm estate in Campbeltown, Scotland. The London home is a large unpretentious but very desirable property of 16 rooms that they've turned into an urban farm. The extensive garden is alive with dogs, ducks, chickens and other pets with a flourishing vegetable patch—important as neither eat much meat. Inside is the clutter of family life and the expensive playthings of the wealthy young man. It has neither the *nouveau riche* vulgarity nor the precious, heavily guarded treasures of many rock musicians. This is because money is nothing new to Linda, nor are the things it buys and anyway, both of them have a relaxed attitude to life. Paul's philosophy is simple: "I like my home to have the things I want in it. It's a happy place, not a museum."

Scotland is their bolt-hole away from the inevitable pressures of a hectic metropolitan and international life. The estate is farmed and carries approximately 150 sheep, in which the McCartneys take a great interest, particularly during the shearing and lambing seasons. However, they are squeamish farmers and will not have their beasts slaughtered. "Every year, Linda and I try to breed them," he told an interviewer. "We do it scientifically, as far as we can. We try to keep them down to 30 lambs a year, by keeping the ewes behind a fence—but that's unless one of the rams leaps over the fence."

He'll wax long and lyrical about the delights of rustic life. All the family ride and Linda is an enthusiastic and successful gardener. She's firmly pro-organic foods untouched by chemical additives and healthy living and describes herself as a country girl at heart. Although raised in New York, she feels no particular pull towards it. "If I lived in America I'd live probably in the desert," she once told *Melody Maker*. "I wouldn't go back to New York City. I like the earth too much. I think so much of life can be seen if you sit in a field."

In several interviews she's insisted that the fame and money, the influence and privilege mean little to her. "Money should not govern your life," she asserted in *Sounds*. "I always said if we lose everything what's the worst that could happen? I like cooking so we'll open a little restaurant."

Linda and Paul are both insistent that the family stays together as much as possible. And that means on the road as well as at home. Right from the first University tour they've taken the children along with them in caravans or coaches. Sometimes the tours are scheduled around school holidays but this is often impossible so a tutor is taken along (in addition to the inestimable Rose, the McCartney's nanny/housekeeper enshrined in *Red Rose Speedway*) to ensure they don't fall behind in their lessons. They have been criticized for what some see as neglect of their children's education but Paul is quick to spring to their own defence. "The kids learn a lot on tour," he told the *Sunday Times*. "But most of all, they have us, they're secure in a family atmosphere. I see these kids in our neighborhood coming home from boarding school and they have just no connection with their families. They're strangers."

McCartney's views on education are individualistic. He sets far more by a person's character than the school at which he or she was educated. He set forth his opinion in *Record Mirror*: "I know a lot of people who are great people and yet not very educated. I also know a lot of people who are very educated and sods. It's learning about life that's important, that's the thing."

If nothing else, the McCartney kids will know a lot about life after their jaunts with the band. The culmination of the McCartney home/business policy came with the Wings Over America tour. They prepared carefully in advance so that they could spend as much time with the children as possible. To this end they rented or borrowed four houses (in Dallas, New York, Chicago and LA), each strategically positioned to be within easy flying distance of a number of venues. These became headquarters for the west, middle and east of the States. During the day the family relaxed together, in the evening Linda cooked a meal and the children went off to bed. Then Linda and Paul flew off to their night's work. After the concert they did a few interviews, fulfilled their duties, hopped back in the plane and slept at the rented house. It was a considerate, loving and sane way of undertaking what could be a fraught, divisive and pressured series of engagements.

If there's such a thing as a truly fulfilled man, then Paul McCartney must come close to being one. He has not only survived, he has prospered, flourished and progressed. He has also had the unusual satisfaction of having been proved publicly right. It is a fitting end to a story that started in acrimony and disharmony to note that seven years after he left the Beatles because he did not want Allen Klein as his manager (years in which he took the brunt of the blame for the rupture) the other three severed their connection with him.

In January, 1977, it was reported that George, John and Ringo had settled

EMI

with Klein out of court. The three agreed to pay their former manager $5,009,200 (about £3,000,000) and as a result all outstanding international legal actions—for fees, commission and expenses allegedly incurred by his company while acting on their behalf—would be dropped. It may have given Paul satisfaction but it was cold financial comfort because, he claimed to a newspaper, some of that enormous sum was his. Any money he had earned up until *Band On The Run* was paid into Apple, some of it had inevitably gone into paying the settlement.

However, it was no time for recriminations. The Beatles were all friends again, they talked on the phone and met regularly. The bitter words of yesterday were forgiven, if not entirely forgotten. There was only one thing in connection with them that ruffled McCartney's calm—the persistent questions: Will the Beatles re-form? Will they play together again?

How ever many times he frankly told reporters that he didn't know, that nothing was impossible, that no-one had definitely ruled it out, that there were no plans just at the moment, that they were not accepting £25,000,000 to do just one show, the questions still kept on coming.

In the end, irritated beyond endurance but still retaining that characteristic sense of humor, he resorted to a parody of another of the world's great personalities—Muhammad Ali. Let it suffice:

The Beatles split in '69
And since then they have been doing fine.
And if that question doesn't cease
Ain't no one gonna get no peace.
And if they ask it just once more
I think I'll have to bash their jaw.

APPENDIX

Text of Paul McCartney interview issued to coincide with release of *McCartney* album, April 1970. 'Interview' consists of questions put by members of the Apple press office.

Q: Why did you decide to make a solo album?

A: Because I got a Studer 4 track recording machine at home—practiced on it (playing all instruments)—liked the results and decided to make it into an album.

Q: Were you influenced by John's adventures with the Plastic Ono Band, and Ringo's solo LP? (1)

A: Sort of but not really.

Q: Are all the songs by Paul McCartney alone?

A: Yes sir.

Q: Will they be so credited: McCartney?

A: It's a bit daft for them to be Lennon/McCartney-credited so "McCartney" it is.

Q: Did you enjoy working as a solo?

A: Very much. I only had me to ask for a decision, and I agreed with me. Remember Linda's on it too, so it's really a double act.

Q: What is Linda's contribution?

A: Strictly speaking she harmonizes, but of course it's more than that because she is a shoulder to lean on, a second opinion, and a photographer of renown. More than all this, she believes in me—constantly.

Q: Where was the album recorded?

A: At home, at EMI (no. 2 studio) and at Morgan Studios (Willesden!)

Q: What is your home equipment (in some detail)?

A: Studer 4 track machine. I only had, however, one mike, and, as Mr Pender, Mr Sweatenham and others only managed to take six months or so (slight delay) I worked without VU meters or a mixer, which meant that everything had to be listened to first (for distortion, etc . . .) then recorded. So the answer—Studer, 1 mike and nerve.

Q: Why did you choose to work in the studios you chose?

A: They were available. EMI is technically good, and Morgan is cosy.

Q: The album was not known about until it was nearly completed. Was this deliberate?

A: Yes, because normally an album is old before it comes out. (aside) Witness *Get Back*. (2)

Q: Why?

A: I've always wanted to buy a Beatles album like 'people' do and be as surprised as they must be. So this was the next best thing. Linda and I are the only two who will be sick of it by the release date. We love it really.

Q: Are you able to describe the texture or the feel of the theme of the album in a few words?

A: Home, Family, Love.

Q: How long did it take to complete—from when to when?

A: From just before (I think) Xmas, until now. *The Lovely Linda* was the first thing I recorded at home, and was originally to test the equipment. That was around Xmas.

Q: Assuming all the songs are new to the public, how new are they to you? Are they recent?

A: One was 1959 (*Hot As Sun*) two from India, *Junk*, *Teddy Boy*, and the rest are pretty recent. *Valentine Day, Momma Miss America*, and *OO You*, were ad-libbed on the spot.

Q: Which instruments have you played on the album?

A: Bass, drums, acoustic guitar, lead guitar, piano and organ-Mellotron, toy xylophone, bow and arrow.

Q: Have you played all these instruments on earlier recordings?

A: Yes—drums being the one that I wouldn't normally do.

Q: Why did you do all the instruments yourself?

A: I think I'm pretty good.

Q: Will Linda be heard on all future records?

A: Could be; we love singing together, and have plenty of opportunity for practice.

Q: Will Paul and Linda become a John and Yoko?

A: No, they will become Paul and Linda.

Q: Are you pleased with your work?

A: Yes.

Q: Will the other Beatles receive the first copies?

A: Wait and see.

Q: What has recording alone taught you?

A: That to make your own decisions about what you do is easy and playing with yourself is difficult but satisfying.

Q: Who has done the artwork?

A: Linda has taken all the photos, and she and I designed the package.

Q: Is it true that neither Allen Klein nor Abkco have been nor will be in any way involved with the production, manufac-

turing, distribution, or promotion of this new album?

A: Not if I can help it.

Q: Did you miss the other Beatles and George Martin? Was there a moment, e.g., when you thought: "Wish Ringo was here for this break"?

A: No.

Q: Assuming this is a very big hit album, will you do another?

A: Even if it isn't, I will continue to do what I want—when I want to.

Q: Are you planning a new album or single with the Beatles?

A: No.

Q: Is this album a rest away from the Beatles or the start of a solo career?

A: Time will tell. Being a solo means it's "the start of a solo career" . . . and not being done with the Beatles means it's a rest. So it's both.

Q: Have you any plans for live appearances?

A: No.

Q: Is your break with the Beatles, temporary or permanent, due to personal differences or musical ones?

A: Personal differences, business differences, musical differences, but most of all because I have a better time with my family. Temporary or permanent? I don't know.

Q: Do you foresee a time when Lennon/McCartney becomes an active songwriting partnership again?

A: No.

Q: What do you feel about John's peace effort? The Plastic Ono Band? Giving back the MBE?(3) Yoko's influence? Yoko?

A: I love John and respect what he does—it doesn't give *me* any pleasure.

Q: Have you any plans to produce any other artists?

A: No.

Q: Were any of the songs on the album originally written with the Beatles in mind?

Capitol

Capitol

A: The older ones were. *Junk* was intended for *Abbey Road,* but something happened. *Teddy Boy* was for *Get Back*(2) but something happened.
Q: Were you pleased with *Abbey Road?* Was it musically restricting?
A: It was a good album. (No. 1 for a long time.)
Q: What is your relationship with Klein?
A: It isn't. I am not in contact with him, and he does not represent me in *any* way.
Q: What is your relationship with Apple?
A: It is the office of a company which I part-own with the other three Beatles. I don't go there because I don't like offices or business, especially when I am on holiday.
Q: Have you any plans to set up an independent production company?
A: McCartney Productions.
Q: What sort of music has influenced you on this album?
A: Light and loose.
Q: Are you writing more prolifically now? or less so?
A: About the same. I have a queue waiting to be recorded.
Q: What are your plans now? A holiday? A musical? A movie? Retirement?
A: My only plan is to grow up.

(1) Ringo had released his first solo album, *Sentimental Journey,* on March 27 in UK and April 24/1970 in US.
(2) *Get Back* was the working title for the movie and album that emerged as *Let It Be* later in 1970.
(3) John Lennon had returned his MBE award in November 1969. In letters to the Queen and the British Prime Minister he said: "I am returning this MBE in protest against Britain's involvement in the Nigeria-Biafra thing, against our support of America in Vietnam and against *Cold Turkey* slipping down the charts."